MASTURBATION MONDAY

MASTURBATION MONDAY

A Shameless Experiment in Self-Love

By Jupiter's Slut

PUBLISHED BY TIPPED EIGHT PRESS

"You are the most powerful person in your life. You are the locus of change."
—JUPITER

Edited by Rachel Kramer-Bussel, Lynsey G, and Meredith Tennant
Cover Design by Laura Duffy
Typesetting by Mark Karis
Author photograph by Erika Kapin

Copyright © 2018 Jupiter's Slut, All rights reserved.

This is a work of nonfiction. The events and experiences detailed herein are rendered as the author experienced and remembered them to the best of her ability. Some names, identities and circumstances have been changed in order to protect the privacy and/or anonymity of the various individuals involved.

All rights reserved. No part of this publication may be reproduced or transmitted in any form or by any means, electronic or mechanical, including photocopying, recording or any information storage or retrieval system now known, or to be invented, without written permission from the publisher.

This edition first published in print format in the United States in 2018.

Tipped Eight Press
351 Pleasant Street
Ste. B #226
Northampton, MA 01060
www.tippedeightpress.com

Digitally designed in the United States of America
First Edition
ISBN: 978-1-7325449-1-8

To anyone who has ever been ashamed to touch themselves.

CONTENTS

1	*not me*	3
2	*mom's advice*	7
3	*home alone*	11
4	*kinky wife*	14
5	*a cowardly cougar*	22
6	*the plan*	28
7	*two fails and a carrot*	33
8	*sex with aliens*	42
9	*v-day*	53
10	*moon boobs*	62
11	*purple penis eater*	69
12	*birthday cock & ass love*	78
13	*mile-high madness*	86
14	*mommy's new toy*	91
15	*invisibilized*	97
16	*i love you, daddy*	106
17	*self-edited*	111
18	*camera whore*	123
19	*ice dragon*	132
20	*teabagging*	140
21	*traffic jam*	145
22	*lost*	149
23	*i need therapy*	161
24	*a gift to the world*	169
	epilogue	175
	about the author	176

"I CAN'T SAY WHY God forbids masturbation," my dad said. "It's not explained. But, if I had to guess, it's probably because masturbation makes you selfish."

I understand why God forbids premarital sex, but I don't understand the prohibition on masturbation, not that I want to do anything like that. I look around the old church. It's dark and cavernous, the high, brown-beamed ceiling and wood-paneled walls eat the light.

Something doesn't seem right about Dad's logic, but I can't say what.

1

not me

I'M DRINKING WITH THE BOYS in the back of the van. The sound of gravel under the tires lulls me like white noise now that we're in the boatyard. Josh takes a turn too fast. I slurp spilled beer from my fingers in the dark and wonder how long until the drinking is done. I'm in it for the sex with my not-exactly-boyfriend Pete. We never do it until the beer is gone.

Boats in dry dock tower overhead. We pass through shadows and between supports that look as thin as twigs under the girth of the hulls. It's a small town, but I love it. The downtown is quaint with turn of the century brick facades, ivy cliffs and a seabreeze. That's where we usually drink. The boatyard is closer to the papermill, whose stink keeps the beaches here empty and pristine.

The van lurches to a stop.

"Get Victor," Pete says.

"Blow me," Tate replies, his chuckle turning into drunk giggles.

We try the horn and wait. Josh gets out of the driver's seat with a huff and slams the door. I picture him climbing the ladder in the dark and the wind. I stay in the warmth of the van. I can't see the ladder lashed to the rail of the boat, but that's the way they do it in dry dock. Between the keel, hull and railing, there's a surprising amount of upkeep to a boat once it's out of the water. No thanks. I'm not jealous of Victor's boat-sitting gig. The wooden ladders are too bendy and too small. Even by day they make me nervous.

I take another swig of cheap beer. It's watery and warm. Good thing I have a high tolerance for pain, because chugging this piss is tonight's prelude to pleasure.

The back door of the van flies open.

"You took forever, dude. You jacking it, or what?" Tate asks.

"Fuck yeah," Victor says with a grin.

"Beer to wash the salami down?" Pete asks. He passes a can to me. I pass it to Victor.

"Every day, all day. You want to jack it for me?" Victor asks.

"No dude, keep it in your pants," Tate says. Tate acts like he's five. I think he's eighteen, like me, but maybe he's older, like Pete and Victor. These aren't town boys, and I am most definitely a town girl. The engine starts. I listen to the gravel under the tires in the night as we head out of the boatyard and to the beach. I expect the conversation to turn to dick size. "I couldn't find it if I tried" is the comeback Tate should have given. These guys are always talking about each other's dicks.

"How often do you masturbate, chica?"

It takes me a minute to realize Victor is talking to me. I'm startled.

"I don't," I say, blushing in the dark.

"What?" asks Tate. "You gotta be kidding."

"I don't," I repeat.

"Liar," says Victor. "Everyone masturbates."

"I don't get the urge," I say. I'm not lying. I just don't, because I don't. I had a wet dream once, a few years ago. I woke riding my pillow. Maybe there was one other time, with a mirror. But I don't masturbate like any kind of regular thing. I don't touch myself down there at all if I can help it.

My not-boyfriend, Pete, usually dominates the conversation, but he doesn't chime in that I don't orgasm either. This is a nonissue, which is probably why he never teases me about it. Instead he mocks me for my faith and my father.

After going to the church for a Free Food Wednesday one week, Pete described my dad, from his Birkenstocks to his one yellowed tooth.

"Yup, that's him," I confirmed.

"The way you talk about your dad, I expected him to be some kind of awesome presence, but he was just, like, a regular dude. Kinda preachy and pathetic," said Pete. Sometimes my dad preached on soup-kitchen nights at church. Gutter punks like getting free shit and mocking anyone who tries to save them. My dad was apparently a big disappointment.

I imagined Pete on his skateboard, leaving the church in the dark, five extra dollars in his pocket for beer. He shook his head and wondered how a smart girl like me could let such an ordinary man hold so much power over her. I was at a loss for words to explain. I thought of what it was like to prepare for my first Communion, my father watching over me. It's not the religion that I value but the skill of introspection. My father taught me to examine myself. I spent years and years examining my heart for any hint of jealousy, non-repentance, greed and every other bad thing. I hated the fear of finding something bad inside me, but I learned something in the looking. I haven't gone to church in a few years. I stopped going around fifteen, but it's still a part of me. Introspection sounds like nothing, but it isn't. It's the best thing about me.

Pete knows my parents divorced when I was three and that my dad traded an alcohol-and-drug addiction for a new one. He's a Jesus freak, saying hallelujah and passing out pamphlets in the streets. I guess I did too good a job describing how important my dad is to me; maybe Pete wanted my dad to be that impressive to him too. My dad doesn't know about Pete, but my mom does. She gets apoplectic at the thought of him. He's twenty-two to my eighteen, and drunk all the time. I haven't introduced him to either of my parents, but I don't keep secrets from my mom.

I don't really talk to my dad much anymore. I see him a couple times a month but we never discuss scripture like we used to. Pete and I argue about free will and destiny in much the same way my dad and I used to discuss the difference between phileo and agape love. We are embarking on another night of drunkenness, just the two of us, out past the boat school.

"Do you have a destiny or not?" Pete badgers me.

"I believe in free will," I tell Pete. "But that doesn't mean I don't believe in destiny too. They aren't mutually exclusive," I explain.

Pete shakes his head. "You can't have both," he says. But he isn't taking a stand for one over the other. We aren't drunk enough yet. I straddle beachwood and pull my jean jacket tight against the breeze and take another swig.

The stars are beautiful. I love living on the water, with a thousand beaches and a million potential castles in the sand.

2

mom's advice

THE PAYPHONE LIGHT ruins my night vision, leaving me completely blind to the darkness beyond. I have no idea if anyone's watching me. Tears stream down my face. It rings. I want to talk to my mom. But it rings, and rings.

"You've reached the home of…"

I try not to cry harder. "Hi, Mom, it's me. I'm not feeling well, um"—my throat constricts—"I'll call again soon. I love you."

I walk to my apartment as bowlegged as I can manage. I'm the most miserable excuse for a cowboy. It hurts. It hurts down there, between my legs. My face is still damp with tears. I take the stairs slow and grip the rail tight. I open the door to my room and go to bed.

I still have a fever in the morning. I'm scared. I get the route map and find a bus to Charity Hospital. I'm nineteen with a minimum-wage job and no health insurance.

My voice cracks as I tell the reception lady why I'm here. I don't want to say out loud where the sores are, but I can't just say "I have a fever." That's not enough reason to go to the emergency room.

A row of chairs lines the waiting room walls. Fluorescent light fills the dingy rectangle of space. I wait. Even just sitting, my pussy is a dull, flaming throb. I don't want to sit here but I'm not looking forward to walking to an exam room. It hurts worse when I walk.

I expect to see blood and gunshot wounds. That's what an inner-city ER is supposed to be like, on TV. It's quiet, though, except for the rustling of seats in chairs and magazines in hands. The slow tick of the clock on the wall is as grating as the tears choking the back of my throat. After a few hours I check back in with the reception lady.

"Do you have any idea how long it will be before I'm seen?" I ask. I'm as polite as I am desperate. I know what triage is; they have to see people according to the severity of their injuries, and all I've got is symptoms.

Six hours later I go home unseen.

I'm faint with fever, and alone. I make my way back to the bus and go home. I'm trembling.

A few days later I find my way to a health clinic. The patient doctor tells me it looks like herpes, but he'll take a swab of the sores just to make sure. There's no medicine for it. I just have to wait. It will get better on its own, eventually. I think of the man who went down on me at the strip club where I'd been working Sunday nights. I'd have been contagious then. I picture a cold sore on his lip. I hope not; he's going through a divorce. That's hard enough. He doesn't need more grief and shame. He's a nice guy.

I go home with a pamphlet in my hand and an empty feeling.

mom's advice

I find my only relief in the bath, my legs splayed over opposite sides of the tub. I spend a few days submerged, wishing the water would never get cold. It does, though, and I drain just enough to warm it again, the hot water a fleeting comfort. I limit movement, so nothing touches the sores. It's like the worst flu I've ever had plus a pussy full of pain. And I'm bored. I wish I could go to work, at my day job. I almost miss the smell of popcorn, but apparently they can live without me at the movie theater for a week or two.

I'm lucky I don't get fired.

New Orleans is two thousand six hundred and ninety-five miles from home, but my mom's voice is right here. A few weeks ago, I stood at the payphone down the street, alone in the dark. Now there's a phone in the apartment. I got a hand-me-down from a woman at work I've been doing some babysitting for. The curly cord is kinked but it's push-button, not rotary. I'm lucky there's a phone jack in my bedroom. I lie on the floor absorbed in the closeness to home. I don't have furniture yet, but I'll find some. The brown shag rug enjoys my fond regard, like a cat that never needs a litter box. I cuddle close. I'm glad it's here for me.

"I'm not going to have sex again until I'm married," I tell my mom. I don't ever want anyone to get as sick as I've been. Herpes is incurable, and there will be a risk of transmitting it for the rest of my life. My heart trembles and breaks. I'm staring down a sentence of celibacy and I have no idea how much time I'm going to serve.

"What am I going to do if I get an urge?" I ask weakly.

"Masturbate," my mother says.

I want to take the phone from my ear. I hate her advice. She might be right but I feel like I need to wipe my ear. Yick. I keep my protestations to myself. *She's probably right,* I think with a shudder. I try to listen because I'm grateful she was home to answer the phone. Petty annoyances, like the stupid advice you don't want to hear, seem relatively benign. But I do not want to masturbate. Ever.

I get urges. I get urges for a man, not for my fingers.

"You should masturbate," I tell myself in the coming weeks. I try once or twice. I have to force my hand down there. I feel stupid. And dumb. I don't know how to do it. And I don't want to. I don't want to, I don't want to.

I wish I didn't have any hormones.

3

home alone

"BARNEY!" my two-year-old yells.

My anti-Barney sentiments have ebbed to an alarming low. Anything is better than *Teletubbies*. Of the three videos we own, *Blue's Clues* is my favorite. I've developed a crush on Steve. But I don't expect my daughter to watch the same thing over and over, not any more than she already does. I pop the video in. Gears turn and the insipid song starts; a child's tolerance for repetition is astonishing.

I sing along, changing the lyrics at will. My perfect bundle of curiosity is absorbed in the nine-inch screen. We're both happy. I hear the word "sensation" and lie on the bed beside her. I'm so tired. I could use a break from any and all sensation.

I startle. My leg jerks and my heart lurches. Shit, I must have fallen asleep. I wipe drool from the corner of my mouth. My girl is still lost in Barneyland. I blink. It's our favorite song, the one I sing wrong all the time. I hear my version in my head: "I smell you, you smell me, we're a stinky family. With a great big zerbert[1] and a zit from me to you…" I lose my inspired thread of improvisation, but there's a "Scooby-Doo" in there somewhere.

Much of my mothering time is spent making up silly ditties to get my girl to brush her teeth or put on her shoes. My mind now works in terms of "tinkles" for potties and sugar-coated little phrases like "oopsie poopsies." But she's totally worth a brain of mush. She's my world.

My husband's gone half the time. He's a hardworking man and the respected captain of a tall ship. When he's gone, I get to have things my way. I turn up the heat. I eat meat. I watch contraband television with my daughter. A forty-five-minute break from the onslaught of 24/7 mothering is a blessed relief.

I fall asleep putting my daughter to bed most nights. She wakes me in the morning. We co-sleep. I don't masturbate; I'm too exhausted. And why would I? It's not like I don't get enough sex. He always makes love to me before he goes, and when he gets back.

My husband is a wonderful man. He's practically a saint.

I try to be a good person too. Before I met him, I canvassed for Greenpeace and volunteered to build latrines in Latin America. We eat organic and I hang the laundry on the clothesline instead of using the dryer, to save the environment the tolling effects of a few more watts of electricity. I cook every meal from scratch, and when he's home it's always vegetarian.

I try so hard. So does my husband. We are both on a quest to be good, worthy people, even after shedding the churches we

---

[1] This is slang for placing one's mouth on skin and blowing out, often to tickle or play. It is also commonly called a raspberry or blowing raspberries.

were raised in. I never say no in bed. I always want sex more than he does. Our lovemaking is sweet and wholesome. He's patient. He's the only man I've ever had an orgasm with.

I imagine his love pouring into me during sex. Alternately, I imagine getting pregnant. I want a baby so bad, it's literally orgasmic. I want children—plural—but he had a vasectomy against my will, when our daughter was only two months old. I imagine the surgery didn't take. My sexual fantasies are of an accidental pregnancy. After seven years, the fantasy sours. I still want a baby, but I stop believing there's any chance I'll ever get pregnant again. Knowing that he's shooting blanks isn't a turn on. As he nears forty, his libido dwindles. It's a normal part of aging, he tells me.

Even as his sexual interest wanes, I do not touch myself. The idea horrifies me as much as shouting, "You aren't sexually satisfying me." And that isn't true. As a good wife, I am satisfied and happy. I make it my job to be satisfied with my life and with my husband. If I'm horny, I wait. Welcome home sex is one of the best parts of being married to a sailor.

4

Kinky Wife

"SEX FAIR." The words on the poster are impossible to ignore, like caution tape around a crime scene. I can't keep my eyes from looking for more. I walk past the door. I can't go inside; I'm a *mom*. I turn red just thinking about it. But it's right there, in the student center. It's Valentine's Day fun, college-style. I'm in college, even if, at twenty-eight, I'm considered a "nontraditional" student because of my age.

I go in.

A wide circle of tables rings the room. At each table, one or two people sit behind displays. Students mill around the middle, asking questions and laughing. I try to look casual like them. I walk past the condoms; I don't need those. I pause at a table with "toys" on it.

"What is this?" I ask.

"It's a vibrating cock ring," she explains. I put it down. I pick up her business card.

"I didn't know we had a sex store in town," I say.

"Yes," she says. "It's by the consignment shop on Maple."

"I know the building," I tell her, "but I've never noticed

your store."

"We're there," she says. "My mother and I opened it two years ago."

Her mother and her. The words thunk down. This isn't some seedy place. I look at her, no longer listening to whatever conversation we're having. She has a warm friendly smile and long hair. If I'd had to guess where she worked based on her clothes I'd have said a new-age bookstore, or the food co-op. She looks like someone I could have known my whole life. I resolve to go into that store soon, before Valentine's Day. I'll buy a gift for my husband.

I park in front of the Lebanese restaurant and pass a clothing shop for kids. I nervously look about. The store is called Oh My, and I don't see it. I'm sure everyone knows what I'm looking for and is judging me. The sidewalk is unbelievably long as I trudge past the other shops. Around the corner I spot a sign with the witty, understated name on it.

I take a breath and head toward the door. Each step is heavy with mortified disbelief, as if garish sexuality dripped from the awning. It doesn't. It's all in my head. I'm freaked by going into a sex shop. They don't use the phrase "sex shop," but I'm sweating like they do. I watch my fingers turn the brass handle. The nondescript outside of the "sensuality" shop gives way to a tasteful inside. The shop radiates a certain boutique sophistication that fits the ethos of the town. I'd be totally comfortable if there weren't sex toys everywhere, and penis-shaped novelties.

I have no idea what to look for. My heart is beating kind of fast. My eyes flit from shelf to shelf; I can't find an easy place to rest them. Everywhere my gaze lands I see something embarrassing. And I have no idea what I want. I just came because…I don't know why. I want to spice things up, I guess. I haplessly pick a porno to rent: low commitment, and cheap. Plus, I get to return it in a few days. The idea of finding a safe place to keep porn or sex toys in the house stresses me out.

I've never watched porn on purpose. In high school I stopped by Norm's house once while he had a porno playing in the background. He was another friend of my not-boyfriend, Pete. I tried to play it cool, like I hardly even noticed. I probably looked as bug-eyed as I felt. In a few minutes, I'd seen enough. The quality of the acting was disappointing. That's an understatement. And I was hurt.

I'd thought the things Pete said when we had sex were unique. But now it sounded like he'd memorized the soundtrack to a porno, maybe this exact porno. I recognized certain phrases. I was sure the same VHS tapes circulated between him and his friends. That was my first step in realizing I was nothing special for Pete.

A decade later, I'm ready to give porn a second chance. I'm excited. This will be an excellent Valentine's Day surprise. Except I have no idea how to choose a porno. I want to ask how, but I know that's stupid. You don't ask how to pick a flavor of ice cream, or a book at the library. I'm overwhelmed.

"Any you recommend?" I ask. She looks a little taken aback. Oh my God. I must sound like such an idiot.

"Depends on what you like," she says.

"I don't know," I say. I am dying.

"Well," she says. I can tell I'm not giving her enough information to go on. "If you like girl/girl this one is popular." A shiny DVD case flashes by with fake-looking boobs busting out of tops. "If you are interested in anal…"

A series of DVD cases blurs across my vision. Her words wash over me. I have no idea what she's talking about. I already said I don't know what I like. She's being really nice, though. I notice one on the shelf with only pregnant ladies. Is that a thing? My brain hurts. I say yes to the next one she holds up. It has a haunted house–type mansion on the front. I'm done.

Calmness settles over me at the cash register. I know how this part of the transaction goes: give money and go home. It's good to be back in familiar territory. She puts my rental in an opaque bag. I walk out the door and into the sunshine. I'm giddy. I float to my car knowing that no one would guess what's in my hand. I'm such an edgy wife. I smile like the wild girl I was before I got married. How did I get so far from her? That girl would have mustered a brazen front, come in wearing fishnets and asked about everything.

What is it about being a wife and a mother that makes me so scared?

I have a fuck ton more to lose now, I guess.

I have to find a hiding place where neither my husband nor daughter will find it. I look around our bedroom: messy bed, messy bookshelves, full laundry hamper. I keep the video in the bag and tuck it on the high shelf in the closet. Valentine's Day will be interesting this year.

"Happy Valentine's Day," I tell my husband with a sweet little kiss. The pretty pink and red wrapping falls away as his strong fingers free the DVD. We watch the porno in bed. I stroke his cock. He's rock hard. The porno is weird. Fascinating and repulsive at the same time. A mad scientist and his lab assistant get to fuck a whole squad of lithe young women dressed like they're in high school. It's a mishmash of genres. It's not realistic; a real scientist wouldn't have a cock piercing. But I'm enjoying it anyway. Half my mind chatters that no girls in the world would wait in line to ride a cock unless they were well paid. But the other half of my mind just stares in drop-jawed admiration. How is it that people get to do this?

I'm pleased with myself and the little spice I've added to the marriage bed. A girl should get good and fucked on Valentine's Day, especially one who's been married eight years.

I think it's going to be a new holiday tradition, The Annual Valentine's Day Porno, but after the second year he says he feels icky watching that stuff. He'd rather I just rent a romantic comedy for Valentine's Day. I thought the porno last year was scary and wondrous. This year, I rented *Pirates XXX*, the porno version of *Pirates of the Caribbean*. Parts of it were filmed on the *HMS Bounty II*. We had friends on the ship's crew, though they hadn't been there during the filming. I just wanted to critique the sailing, see what they did on the boat. Most of the sex was stupid, and the women didn't even look like they enjoyed it. But there was one scene where the woman broke character and was actually having a genuinely good time. You could tell; she was smiling radiantly. I liked that. It made me happy. But the hottest scene was one with a woman tied to a chair, legs open, no panties. I can't get that out of my head. She was so exposed.

I'd hoped the pornos would spark some discussion of sexual fantasies, but apparently even a single smut session per year is too much. Maybe he's right; it does make me feel a little icky. It's just, that's not all it makes me feel. And I want to talk about our sexual fantasies. Nothing else I've said or asked seems to get that conversation off the ground.

I used to imagine his love filling me, like a million pearls of swimming light. I used to imagine his vasectomy didn't take and that this time I'd get pregnant. I put the odds around those of getting struck by lightning. But people *do* get struck by lightning. I want a baby and I can't have one unless I go to a sperm bank. The idea of carrying someone else's child makes me sick. The idea of explaining to my children why they don't have the same father makes me sick.

We aren't having sex as much as we used to.

I masturbate, some. I imagine I'm on a boat. The entire crew wants to fuck me. They circle up around me on deck. I'm spread-eagle on a hatch as I take one cock after another. Oh God, yes. They *want* me.

I am disturbed by my fantasy. And I feel guilty.

One time I ask my husband to watch me touch myself. I find this to be the most excruciating humiliation, him seeing me down there. And seeing me touch myself, attempting to give myself pleasure. He says it's a huge turn-on, but he never asks me to do it again. I find it harder to orgasm during sex. I'm bored. My mind wanders.

It shouldn't be like this.

And it gets worse.

I imagine being raped. I imagine it and masturbate. I imagine it and don't even touch myself. I can't sleep at night. I get up, lace on my sneakers and run in the dark. Sometimes the homeless sleep in the brush beside the old rail trail where I run. I don't care if I'm raped. Maybe I'll get pregnant.

I scare myself.

I don't think on these things. I'm a glass-half-full kind of girl, but sorrow springs up in horrible places, like when he smiles to congratulate someone else on expecting a child.

I try. I talk. I explain. I read books and buy lingerie. I get counseling again and again. Rather than being critical, I should be loving. I pour my love into him. For a few days at a time, we perk up. The counselor says to work on *me*. I can't change him, but if I change me, then he'll change too. I try to never be critical. I try to accept exactly who he is and love him for it.

I graduate in the top twenty-five percent of my class at Smith College, with departmental and Latin honors. I design a chicken coop to match the house and we raise hens from adorable little balls of fluff. I plant a patch of strawberries in the backyard and mulch it with grounds from the free-trade coffee shop down the street. I put twenty-five feet of raspberries along the south side of the garage. I tuck rhubarb all over the place; that's my favorite.

I drive my daughter to school. After school I help her check the coop for eggs. I start grad school. We raise a guide dog for the blind. We take a week's vacation to hike a small portion of the Appalachian Trail as a family. I finish one graduate degree and start another. I teach middle school math. I never stop wanting another baby. We talk about it and come up with no solutions. We have even less sex.

Hidden sorrows become soul-rending torments. Dedicating my life to finding a way for us to be happy is killing me. Our happiness requires the sacrifice of me, over and over. After thirteen and a half years as a faithful wife, I'm done. I can feel it in my gut. I'm done. We are good together as parents but the marriage is over.

"I'm not asking for a divorce," I tell him, "but I'm taking a lover."

"I hope it helps," he says. "I hope it makes you happy."

To my utter shock, I can't orgasm with my new lover. I thought I was over that. I've been orgasming for over a decade. Am I that embarrassed to have someone new see me orgasm? I mistook familiarity of sex with my husband, for sexual maturity and confidence.

After weeks, eventually I come. It takes lots of trying. I screw my eyes up really tight. I have to put something over the lamp so it's darker. I have to block the chatter in my mind.

"Come for Daddy," he says.

I repeat his words like a mantra. "For Daddy, for Daddy, for Daddy."

The idea of him thinking he couldn't make me orgasm is horrible. I'll give him an orgasm if it kills me.

He tells me to masturbate at home and think of him.

I masturbate to fantasies of every kink he mentions. I want to make him happy, more than anything in the world.

5

a cowardly cougar

I RUSH HOME FROM WORK to catch the last of the afternoon light. I leave the worries of teaching behind as I step out of my clothes. I've been dared to take a full nude.

I put a hand over my groin.

Click. The digital shutter cues, and I change poses.

My arm adds visual interest and hides my little belly.

I angle my head, smile bigger and squeeze the remote control shutter. It's wireless and small enough to disappear like a magic quarter in my hand. I turn toward the camera, for a slimming forty-five-degree angle. My belly wasn't flat before the baby; it still isn't flat fifteen years later. It is cute, though. I'm cute. I mollify myself with a sarcastic affirmation. I am cute enough, I'm smart enough and gosh darn it, I like me. I'm pudgy in a classic artsy way.

It's easy to take a hundred pictures without noticing, with no film to advance between shots. I choose a pic and send it to Jason.

That's his nickname. He's Canadian and of Middle Eastern descent. He thinks no one can pronounce his real name. But I could totally do it, if given a bit of time and practice. I spent a semester in South Korea; my mouth and vocal cords like to try strange new things.

I also spent a month in Ecuador. My Spanish ain't bad for only one year in high school. French too, though it was harder. It took weeks of trying to gargle and talk at the same time before I could roll my Rs, but my tongue can do anything.

Jason's smile kills me. I dream of flying up to Canada and showing him exactly what my tongue can do. I won't, though. I'm not going to have any new relationships until I am legally single, not just separated. But I could.

Would a weekend fling really count as a "relationship"?

My phone vibrates. There's a picture. Jason's in the bathroom, wet and naked but coyly hiding his privates behind a shampoo bottle. This guy may be young, but he's got the art of seduction nailed. I'm a wee bit embarrassed to admit that he's under twenty-five, and a wee bit proud. Who would have guessed I'd grow up to be a cougar? I don't think that was even a thing when I was a kid. Wait, let me think a second. Yeah, never mind. That movie *The Graduate* is like ten years older than I am. Mrs. Robinson is my opposite with her sophisticated ennui. I am inexperienced enthusiasm personified. I am so fucking embarrassing.

I look back at my phone and count his six pack to make sure it's all there. Yup. That's six. Three pairs of two, fully visible. Or two columns of three. Either way, I'm impressed. I didn't think I cared about physique, but I want to lick his hard abs.

Is this kind of fantasy cheating on my commitment to being single?

A video pops up on my phone. Water runs down the corded

muscles of his back and trickles off his elbows. He turns to the camera. Water streams over his chest to the trail of hair above his groin. I didn't used to like muscle guys, but I'm getting over it. Maybe I was too insecure about my plumpness before and was just masking it with disdain for the physically fit. Or maybe tastes just change as we mature? Whatever the reason, damn fucking hell, he's hot.

I play the video clip again. And a third time.

I totally want to fly up for the weekend. I'll wear a little 1950s bikini while he bench-presses me for the camera. I can't believe such a hot guy is interested in me, but lately a bunch of gorgeous men have been coming on to me. I'm getting more used to it, mostly.

I've been filling the void with social media since I moved out. That sounds bad, but it's a step in the right direction. I had two outside lovers in the last years of my marriage; each lasted about a year. I poured myself into loving them. Now that I'm committed to being single, I don't know what to do with all the attention I used to lavish on men.

I've been acting like Instagram is my new lover. I say good morning, post sexy pics randomly through the day and blow a virtual good-night kiss to the world. Followers flock to me. It's delightful.

I don't want to make anyone or any relationship the centerpiece of my life right now. Instagram is *almost* like investing in myself. Some of my social media followers now read my blog. They love my emails and my pictures. That makes me happy. It's a start.

Chat at eight? he asks.

I agree.

I take a shower and show up clean and fresh at eight o'clock. It's practically bedtime. I wear a floral nightgown, sweet and innocent.

"Hi, you made it," he says. His accent is adorable.

It's all I can do to stop myself from squealing in delight. I'm ridiculous. I'm talking to a man more than fifteen years younger than me, and I feel like a schoolgirl.

"Hi," I say.

"How are you?" he asks.

"Feeling a bit shy."

"Are you blushing?" He sounds incredulous.

"Probably." I'm totally blushing, twice as hard now. I can feel it.

"Why are you so shy?"

"I've never done this before." I sound like an idiot. It's not like I'm a virgin.

"You're so cute," he tells me.

I am cute. And ridiculous. I pull the covers over half my face. I want to hide under them but staring at a lump would get boring fast.

"I only have like twenty minutes if I want dinner," he says. The room behind him is small, industrial and clean. It's not homey like a college dorm room. No posters, no pillows.

"Send me a pic of the mess hall, if you don't mind." I'm curious about every aspect of life on an oil field.

"Do you know what the guys will say if I'm taking pictures of my food?"

"Tell them it's for a boobilicious hottie in the States."

"I showed your pic around." He holds up a face shot with my eyes extra-bright blue. "The guys are all jealous."

"I'd like to make them jealous in person," I tell him. Does wishing this count as cheating on my vow of celibacy? Am I aiming at emotional celibacy or just physical?

God, I don't even know.

"I want to see you touch yourself," he says.

I knew that was coming. I'm as nervous as I'd be jumping off a dock with a twenty-foot drop to the water. I used to do that as a kid. It never got less scary.

"Okay," I say.

I tease my nightgown up my leg slowly. I have killer calves.

"You are beautiful," he says.

When my nightgown reaches that special place, where my legs meet, I cover myself with one hand.

"I'm shy," I complain.

"Don't be," he says. He's smiling his beautiful smile. I flick my fingertip at the phone's camera lens, letting just a patch of extra skin show.

"Okay," I say, and ease into what I've known I'm going to do.

I want this.

I pull my pussy lips open wide with my fingers.

"Oh God," he says.

I can't believe he likes what he sees, but I hope it's true.

"You're already wet," he says with a hint of jubilation in his voice.

"I was thinking about you." I'm flushed with desire. It's pricking my skin from face to thighs—and in between.

"Let me see you come."

"I don't always orgasm," I admit, feeling like a super big idiot.

"I know you can do it for me," he says. Somehow, I believe I can do it for him too.

I prop the camera on a pillow and lean back. It's a less awkward angle. I lick my fingers and rub a light circle on my clit, very light. I can hear my breathing start to change as my circling fingers fall into a regular steady rhythm.

"That's beautiful, baby. Just beautiful."

I crane my neck to see his face on the screen. The phone slips on the covers. I prop it up again. I try to show my pussy and my face at the same time. It's not easy. I get it just right and then, oops, knock the camera over again. We laugh. He has a beautiful laugh.

I imagine he's got a fistful of my hair in one hand and is just piercing into me with the tip of his penis for the first time.

"Come for me," he says.

I imagine his face above mine, his chest and the feel of him stroking in and out. I imagine him coming inside me.

"Come for me, baby," he says.

My body clenches in orgasm and my eyes roll. My breasts wobble heavily back and forth.

"That was beautiful, baby," he says. "That was beautiful."

I lie in bed warm with the afterglow of orgasm. He's gone to eat before the mess hall closes. Part of me is going to bed satisfied, the other part is totally mortified. I can't believe I just did that.

No, I *can* believe I just did that. What I can't believe is that I'm almost forty and I'm still ashamed to touch myself.

That has to change.

6

the plan

INTENSE MOANING, obviously on the verge of orgasm, starts the short video clip, but you can't see anything. The screen is dark. I can't believe I'm going to post this on Instagram. Technically it doesn't violate the rules—no nudity. But why am I doing this?

The cool thing about the video is that a really loud airplane buzzed my house as I was recording. It's perfectly timed to my orgasm. I couldn't have mixed the audio that way if I'd tried. I recorded the little video to send to Jason, but he's been distant. I'm going to post it online instead. I press the button and wait. I'm holding my breath.

Why is this so nerve-wracking?

Literally millions of people post sexually explicit pics. From sexting to Fetlife, naughty nudes have become ubiquitous. Obviously other people also enjoy posting sexy stuff. But the assumption is that they are all trailer-park trash, or the urban equivalent…not upstanding people like me. I hold two master's degrees. I am a math teacher. I shake my head at myself. I think of Anthony Weiner. He's also well educated and likes to sext. "Weiner does it," isn't a defense likely to win me friends, especially since he's been caught sexting underage girls.

What will people think of me? That's the terrifying question. What would my daughter's friends' parents think? What would my ex-in-laws think? What about my neighbors? If I were to get a stalker, would the police protect me, or would they treat me like I deserved it? I can hear people's derisive thoughts. *What did she expect, posting that stuff online? She was asking for it.* My stomach clenches.

"Get a grip, me. You aren't on trial," I tell myself. I refresh the app.

I have comments.

That is soooo fucking hot! 🔥🔥🔥
Oh my god, 😍
Just hearing that, holy shit.

More comments scroll across the screen. I've got thirty of them within a few hours, all positive. All of them. My brain is going to explode. I post the most embarrassing things and people love it. The parts of myself I've been trying to ignore, hide and stifle, the rest of the world is loving up. Why do I hate these parts of myself that strangers are so eager to appreciate and encourage?

You are amazing!!!!!!
Check your DMs
I wanna do dat 4 u
You make me so hard, baby 🍆
Vous êtes incroyable 🤍🤍🤍
I love you.

This isn't real love but it's pleasant. I'm surprised, though. Didn't they read *The Scarlet Letter* in high school? I'm supposed to be put in the stocks while jeering crowds throw rotten tomatoes at me. Shouldn't there be some comments calling me a whore? Or at least a cheap attention seeker?

Thank you, you made my day.

أنا أحب كبير الثدي 🤍

#masturbationmonday material
Your orgasm sounds are so cute.
Instant wood! 🥒🥒🥒😈
Suck my cock.

The positivity is almost unrelenting. Well, maybe "positivity" isn't the right word. Is it positive to have everyone saying you turn them on? Does it corrupt? Am I going to get a big ego? I can't reciprocate all this attention. Is that unfair? Am I wronging these men to whet their sexual appetites and leave them hanging? These thoughts creep into my mind. I try not to listen. I enjoyed posting the video. That's a fact. Others enjoyed watching it. That's a fact. I'm not going to think further than that.

I listen to the post again. God, the way the airplane jets rev in unison with the acceleration of the orgasm, it's artistic.

Can it be artistic if it's accidental?

I don't get a comment from Jason. His posts get almost as many comments as mine. He really is a hunk.

How's your day? I message him. *Heading back to the fields soon?*

Yes. Tomorrow.

That's gotta be hard, to leave Princess. I picture him curled up on the couch with his adorable dog, a three-year-old Shepherd mix.

Yeah, it will be.

He doesn't say anything else. No more texts, no good-bye. I'm vaguely puzzled but I'm not going to read too much into a little aloofness.

I give the thread closure with, *I hope you have a wonderful last day with her.*

I'm not a good guy, he texts. Wow, that was a non sequitur. *I'm the kind of guy who has a one-night stand and never calls again*, he explains. *I'm a jerk.*

Okay, I reply. I don't know what else to say. What's he expect me to do with that information? Not date him? For fuck's sake, he's literally a frozen tundra away. Maybe he had a fling and is just feeling down on himself.

I'm disappointed but not surprised when he starts acting like a jerk, making pointed comments and standing me up. I block him.

My goal is to concentrate on me. If I just keep repeating that, maybe it'll come true. I feel a little bad for Jason, though. His mother left him at a young age; clearly he's playing out a pattern. I wish him the best, but spending my time dreaming of flying to Canada to fuck him was a waste of my energy. I'm trying to invest in me. I just don't know how. It's hard.

Being celibate at this point in my life is ironic, with overtones of "it's not fair." I just claimed my sexual freedom. Two years ago, I took a lover out of desperation, I was so sexually starved. Now I'm committing to celibacy? What the fuck am I thinking? I want sex. I want lots of it.

Big sigh.

The lovers I had before I moved out of the family home were also a huge suck of time and energy. They promised the world and delivered nothing, or worse than nothing—they gave lies. I can't stop thinking of what it would be like if I took all the crazy love I lavished on men and channeled it into something that benefited *me*.

I don't ever want to feel used and betrayed like that again. I don't ever want to feel so unheard and taken for granted. I know you have to value yourself if you want others to value you. I just don't know how to value me.

Jesus Christ, I'm not an after-school special. It's not like I don't value and invest in myself. I went to one of the best colleges in the country. I studied my ass off to give myself the best education I could get while I was there.

Then why do I keep choosing such shitty men?

BAHHH! These thoughts make me want to pull my hair out.

I don't know how to survive celibacy when I just got my sexual freedom back.

I guess I should masturbate.

Fucking hell! I hate masturbating. It makes me feel like a loser to have to touch myself. And I don't know how to do it. Sometimes I can't even orgasm. It's hard, and it takes forever. I'd rather have cock. I love cock.

Wow.

I guess I really need to learn how to masturbate.

That's it! I'm going to masturbate at least once a week for a year. I'll make a disciplined practice of it. I'll video the sessions and examine my own sexuality, and the shame. If I post about it on my blog, I won't be able to back out or slack off. People will be expecting my videos. I can use that #masturbationmonday thing! Masturbation Monday. I like the way that sounds. It's got a built-in posting deadline. It's perfect.

I'm brilliant.

7

two fails and a carrot

"HELLO, ME, what will turn you on today?"

Nothing, go away. I'm hairy, tired, bored and lonely. I don't wanna masturbate.

"That's the point of a practice. You do something with commitment because it's more important than your passing whims."

I want someone else to fuck my brains out. But I'm too hairy. Someone could shave me first. Yeah, someone could shave and then fuck me while I just lie here.

"Huh, well. Thanks for being honest. Yeah, I guess you're right. We can't film before we shave."

I said I want to lie back and get fucked. I just want to be passive, unless the switch flips and I go animalistic.

"We are getting in touch with our sexuality, not handing it over to someone else."

Handing it over sounds really good, and damn effing sexy.

"Ha, ha. You are funny."

I'm serious. I just want cock.

"I know. But you aren't going to do that. Listen, we can make it sexy ourselves. We'll shave for the camera. You love the camera. That will make it fun. Two birds with one stone. You appreciate efficiency. It's nifty."

Do I have to?

"Come on!"

Okay, but I kinda hate you.

I drag my ass to the bathroom for the electric razor. I turn my phone to airplane mode so the recording won't be interrupted. The spring-loaded clip holds the phone snugly on the tripod. Video. Okay.

Clouds of inertia drift away. Razor in hand, I look at my calves. I have beautiful legs. I don't like shaving but it's good to see something in myself worth admiring. I look into the camera. Messy hair and a bland unmade face stare back. I haven't showered since dance class and I'm still in my leotard. I brush my hair and begin to brighten.

I'm new to this. I explain myself to the camera. I feel shy and giddy with the camera looking at me. Someone is going to see this video. They'll see me: goobery, sweet, plump, happy me.

It looks as if I'm enjoying shaving my legs, but it's really just the legs I'm enjoying. The shaving is tolerated. My calves are large and shapely in a vá vá vá voom kind of way.

I go ass up and give my future viewers a face full of flat white booty. Sounds raunchy but it's sweet. I'm smiling. My anus comes off as demure somehow and my pussy from this angle is, well, inviting. It's hard to reach around to the scraggly ass hairs, of which there are many. I can't see what I'm doing worth shit. I close my eyes and imagine where the razor is going and what the camera sees. The buzz of the little electric motor says it's doing all the work, but ass-shaving by the guess-and-check method is inordinately exhausting, as is ass-reaching. I move gingerly; I don't want shaving nicks on my ass. I turn the razor off as soon as I can. I'm not saying much to the camera at this point. Creating asstopia has wiped me out.

I cannot fathom trying to pussy-shave after all this fuss.

Nor am I orgasmic.

Failure.

※

I didn't even get fingers to clit while the razor was on. In my mind I can do anything, including rub one out under the buzz of electric hair removal. In my imagination I can also outrun cars. But shaving failed to get me anywhere near orgasm.

Time to regroup and strategize.

Shower break.

Urban legends taught me bathtubs and showers are great for masturbation, but water washes away my natural lubrication. I already have enough doubt about my ability to orgasm. No extra challenges this early on, thank you.

I put my thinking cap on. I'm earnest, silly and innocent, like Winnie the Pooh. *Think, think, think. What will turn me on? If underwater is one of the hardest ways for me to orgasm, what's one of the easiest? Easy. Easy, easy peasy.*

Ah! There was that time I'd been in bed icing an injury and got bored. The ice pack ended up between my legs, producing one exultant orgasm. Creativity + horniness = joy.

I decide that's what I should do in today's masturbation video. I will catalog this method, among many more soon-to-be-discovered methods, as I grow my list of tried and true physical pleasures. Instead of an ice pack I grab an ice cube.

"More direct clitoral stimulation will be all the more

orgasmic," I tell myself while a warm ball of smugness grows in my chest. With an ice cube and a jar of coconut oil, I pounce on the bed. Coconut oil makes my clit super slick and super soft.

I press the ice to myself and want to scream. Jesus H. Motherfucking Christ, this is cold. Water drips down my fingers.

Ahhh.

I whine. This ice cube is *nothing* like the ice pack. The heat of my pussy battles the frozen cube of water. Rivulets run down my labial folds. Fuck. I drop the cube. Too cold.

Alternating hot and cold works like internal massage, flushing toxins from an area, with heat drawing blood in and cold pushing it back out. Expansion and contraction.

I want a special contraction, the big uncontrollable kind that feels expansive.

Despite my complete and utter belief that I'd orgasm from putting ice on my clit, I was wrong. I did not orgasm. And no number of self-applied ice cubes is going to do the deed. Ice cube = ice pack was a misassumption. When I think about it, the surface area covered would make a difference. When I think about it, the conductivity of ice is different than that of an ice pack. Duh. Ice cube ≠ ice pack. I was not thinking. I was assuming and making a mad rush for anything I thought would get an orgasm.

On principle, I strongly object to conceiving of sex as an orgasm-only event.

But right now I really want a fucking orgasm, or I'll totally feel like a failure. Guys always orgasm. It's really frustrating not to know if I am going to be able to climax. It's like I can't count on myself. And I don't know why.

Blech, nasty thoughts.

Failure.

I lie on the bed, close my eyes and clear my mind.

I approach myself anew.

"What do you need to come?"

Something sexy.

"What is sexy?"

I don't know.

"Well, hmm. What do you want?"

I want something down there, inside me.

"Oh-kaay, what do we have for that?" An image of a wine bottle flashes through my mind. Horror. I want something less dangerous, less wanton. More wholesome.

Is there a cucumber in the fridge?

"You are never going to forget that poem, are you? A cucumber is way too embarrassing. People are going to watch whatever we do."

Yes, it is going to be so embarrassing!

Something inside me brightens. My whole body blushes, clit included. I can't believe I'm going to shove a cucumber in myself and commit that act to film. I begrudgingly make my way to the fridge, feeling like an idiot for not owning a dildo. That might have been a good thing to buy right off the bat.

Why am I freaking out? This is supposed to be honest. It's not as if I've never masturbated with a vegetable before. I have. Maybe twice. That hole down there is meant for things to go in and out of it. And when it hasn't had anything in it, in a really long time, that gets kinda problematic. Ironically, if I wasn't so ashamed of sex, I'd never have fucked vegetables. I'd have used a proper dildo. But good girls don't have dildos in the back of their panty drawers. Face it: my genuine attempt at virtue spawned what could rightly be called vegetal depravity.

Maybe that's a bit melodramatic. We could think positively. Vegetables are organic. Making do with what I have makes me kinda proud. Ego boost—my orgasms are free from BPAs and the capitalist machine.

I'm stalling.

I know what is going to turn me on. Either I accept myself or I closet myself. The closet I can't do. I know that. If I could, I'd have stayed married. The choice is already made. I am me. I am apparently a vegetable fucker. I didn't know that before. But now I do, and I'm not going to try to hide it. Who knew unconditional self-love would be so freaky?

I pull the fridge door open. Cold billows out. My nipples grow harder.

There are no cucumbers.

No zucchinis.

Just big fat orange carrots. I grab one. Should I wash and peel it? There are microbes in dirt, even in organic dirt, maybe especially in organic dirt. I'm thinking of how much more embarrassing it would be to get some kind of infection from a garden-variety sex act immortalized on film.

I'll put a condom on it.

I kneel on the bed, jammies open, carrot caressing my tummy as if I were the sexiest thing that ever was. I roll its cool length on my skin, without thinking. I follow the motion of the carrot. In the doing comes the magic, and I surrender. I tickle its little root end at my belly button. Flirtatious energy flows through me; it directs my actions unfiltered. I thunk the hunk of carrot on my breast and await another impulse.

No proper porno skips the blow job. With a flirtatious lick

two fails and a carrot

I tease the carrot, then I bite the tip off. Menacing. I imagine the male audience cringing as they cream themselves. The carrot is cold on my lips. It's amazing how fat this carrot gets. It's not your average grocery store variety. The benefits of supporting local organic farms just don't end. The girth I'm enjoying here is unusual, be it carrot or cock.

I take my time. I know the way my mouth accommodates this phallic root will drive watchers mad. And then I'm done. It's time to get to business. It's time to get selfish. It's time to get a condom on it.

Whoops.

Condoms fly. Right across the room. I don't know how that happened. It was like one of those pop toys.

No matter. I retrieve said condom and wrangle it on to that carrot. I grab the open end of the condom and spin the carrot overhead. Like a helicopter cock, it's going to take me up. I'm smiling like an impish bitch. I can feel it. This carrot is mine. I reward it with little tongue flicks to the tip of its head. I do it because it feels good. I do it 'cause I love to tease. I do it 'cause it pops into my head to do it.

Tick, tock, now I've got a carrot-in-the-condom pendulum. I'm poking fun at myself and being silly but this is, hands down, one of the most embarrassing things I have ever done.

I play coy, then lie back and show the camera. Here is me. Jiggly, wiggly old me. Hello, parts I like. Hello, parts I don't like. I see you. I see me. Anyone who cares to will see all my worst and most intimate parts. My big pussy is shiny and delicate. The folds are all foldy and not at all symmetrical. I'm not hiding it. I look like I've had a baby. It's out there for everyone to see. And it has a carrot going in and out of it now.

Big.
Fat.
Hard.
Thick.
Carrot.

How many men watching this video will wish they were a carrot? Awesome. I am so fucking powerfully awesome. I love my twisted sweet self.

I need more lube.

This carrot is so huge it won't stay in me. I laugh. Does this mean I'm "tight"?

I push the carrot back in and try to anchor it with the condom top wrapped around my finger.

It pops back out. This carrot really doesn't want to stay in there. I keep a finger over its fat butt and pump it in and out. This carrot means business. It's pumping in and out like a little bunny's after it. Carrot thrust in, carrot thrust out.

People are going to think I'm insane.

Breasts bare and soft flannel jammies.

My eyes begin to roll.

I start to huff.

Breath puffing like the little engine that could.

I stop.

I start again.

I can tell when I'm going to come. I get noisy.

Getting noisy turns me on.

I'm going to come.

Oh, yum.

Giggles erupt.

This is silly.

I'm laughing and orgasming.

Sex is silly.

I am silly.

I have to pull the carrot out before the aftershocks of orgasm are finished. It's too much. I am happy. Me and my fat pussy and my big smiles and my body that gives me carrot-juicy orgasm are sated. And that perfectly naughty part of me that knows, in the end, exactly what will turn me on. I just have to listen to the scariest parts of me. It's as easy as a carrot in coconut oil.

Two Fails and a Carrot is an essay inspired by filming and editing of *DMS Ass Shaving, Hydrotherapy Fail* and *Coconut & Carrots,* January 2016.

8

sex with aliens

I'M A SEX-IN-THE-AFTERNOON GIRL, but deadlines dictate that I film this morning. The camera runs while I lie here with a pillow over my head, mentally searching for something sexy. I peek at the camera screen. I've been filming for five directionless minutes with a tissue tucked in the waistband of my jammies. I pull the offending tissue from its cozy spot and throw it out of frame. My grandmother kept tissues tucked in her nightgown sleeve. This is not sexy. I've turned into my grandmother. That thought makes my pussy shrivel and die a little. But it's not my fault. I have allergies. On the bright side, I am quite adept at nose honking. I call it "playing my love horn."

"Back to work, you. You are supposed to think of something sexy to do, not marinate in how innately unsexy you feel right now."

My fingers rub over my clit. My jammy bottoms are soft, pre-loved gray-and-white striped cotton with a satin drawstring at the waist. My mom got them for me at Goodwill. So many layers of love right there. But not so much sexiness. Search brain. Search. Search. Search. Go far. Really far. Intergalactic far.

With a name like Jupiter's Slut, I should have intergalactic sexual fantasies. Seems like something that would be dictated by cosmic law, right? Yeah. I close my eyes and imagine myself on a *Star Wars*–type mission. My swagger is more Lara Croft than Princess Leia despite the fact that my spaceship looks like I stole it from the Jetsons.

Wait, my spaceship looks like what!? Jeez, imagination, cool up. I squeeze my mental muscles real hard and some *Mad Max*-ish spikes pop up on the hood of my spaceship. Okay, better. I'm not completely satisfied but it's time to stop designing my spaceship. Sex. Think sex.

Sex, sex, sex.

What sexy thing could happen to me in space? I'm on a mission. I'm hot. I know how to drive my spaceship so good, I'm, like, super skilled. Bad guys are obviously going to be after me. Some of them have to be sexy, right? That's how romance novels and sci-fi movies work, isn't it? Where would I be going? What situation would land me in the middle of a super-hot sex scene?

Scene: *Buxom blonde roves the galaxy with space-age gun holsters strapped to her thighs and not much else on. With those tits she's a knockout, but her wit is the true enemy of smarmy sexbots everywhere. She zooms through the stars, wagging her untouchable ass in the face of despots and the debonair alike, her eyes focused on freedom and the Universal Way…while running a small but lucrative smuggling gig on the side.*

This could be a graphic novel. I'd love to be serialized as a space-age sexual superhero. I put my hand down my pants and simultaneously stroke my ego and my clit.

Narration: *Sometimes she's on top, sometimes she's on bottom, but she always gets what she wants in the end.*

I can just see the illustration of that double entendre. I'd also love to see a drawing of my spaceship. An illustrator would make it so much more awesome. And I'd love to see a drawing of me shooting a sexbot. He's literally smoldering but I lash him with a wry quip that proves my intellect is as bright and deadly as my laser gun. After I'm done with him, I'd saunter sexily through the space station in search of onion rings and bourbon.

I close my eyes and smell the onion rings on the soft breeze of the space station's oxygen recycling system. There's someone behind me. I feel it a nanosecond after it's too late.

"*No, you don't, Princess.*"

I know that voice. Anger and excitement flood me. Before I can set my laser to singe, his furry face is in front of mine. I can't move. The motherfucker immobilized me! How the hell did he do that?

His eyes are the most beautiful brown. No, no, no. Not him. Anyone but this motherfucker. He slaps hover patches on my shoes, links his arm in mine and starts apologizing, the jerk.

"*I'm sorry, Princess. I'd have asked, but you might have said no. I've got a hell of a client for you.*"

I can't do anything but listen and watch the light glint off his chestnut fur. I'm the biggest traitor I've ever met. How can I find this motherfucker anything but repulsive after all the shit he's put me through?

I won't let myself forget his betrayals. Think of the tears on the Tandirez. *Remember.*

"*He's willing to pay five thousand zitbots for one hour with you.*"

Nothing like a spike of anger to burn off an impractical spell of lust and infatuation. I'd call him a motherfucker out loud but that immobilization device is too strong. I can't even move my mouth.

I wonder how my eyes are still blinking, or my heart still beating. I am going to bite his head off when I'm free. I can't wait. But I motherfucking have to. I strain to move but I'm obviously not doing shit until he chooses. Fucker.

We round a corner. The sign above the docking station says 68B-1. I'm loaded onto a yacht-y cruiser. Fucking swank. Okay, time to clear my head. I've got options. There are always options. I don't do stuck. He knows that. He's testing. He's hoping. And he's oh, so fucking wrong.

Holy shit. The guy behind the desk is gorgeous.

"Alister," Jax says to the guy. "This is Jupiter. She can swallow a cock whole while staring at you with the eyes of a virgin. She loves group sex and can take six cocks at a time."

Goddamn him. He's telling the truth and I'm getting wet from all the talk, the money and the flattery. He knows my weaknesses and he's dangling them in my face, smug fucker. I would have done anything he said once, but not anymore. I captain my own ship now.

"I thought she was a Slut," says the gold-drenched Alister.

"She is," Jax tells him. "She is."

Finally they switch off the immobilizers.

I don't say a word. I just smile and cold cock his whiskered nose. I hear it break. Jax's blood is on my knuckles as I walk away, not even bothering to check Alister's reaction. I can picture his face. It's a funny thing, just knowing I have Proton-5s strapped to my thighs; it's like I give off an unquestionable-confidence vibe. Only Jax would be oblivious to how I've changed. Actually he wasn't entirely, or he wouldn't have immobilized me.

Maybe Jax will think twice next time. I can't believe I had to hold my hand back from helping him up. The look on his face when he felt my fist, it warms and breaks my heart at the same time.

When will I get it through my head? Jax is a motherfucker. He's never going to learn. I need to see red when I look at his silky ears. He's an assuming asshole and he's not going to change.

Funny thing, I'd probably have loved that client if I'd found him myself. Fucking Jax.

I need those damn onion rings, and bourbon…over ice cream.

This fantasy is awesome, but it's not turning me on sexually. I need something else. Something more. I ask my imagination for a scenario that will make me pant and beg.

Scene: *Half a galaxy away and years later, Jupiter's more sophisticated and confident and, if possible, even sexier. She's sipping bourbon and playing Mey Wong with a tentacled stranger. The game pieces float in a sphere of antigravity.*

Narration: *She knows what she wants. She wants what she wants. And her smile makes you wonder if she's going to get it sooner than you think.*

Camera zooms from her succulent ankles to his impenetrable eyes. Dialogue commences.

"I haven't decided if you are a Player or not."

She knew it was Lord Vollner's thought in her mind but otherwise she'd have sworn he was speaking aloud. She wasn't going to let the disconcerting illusion distract her.

"The universe is my playground," Jupiter says. The movements of her mouth feel exaggerated. It's strange talking aloud when she knows she doesn't have to. To anyone watching, it must look like she's talking to herself, but it helps her focus her thoughts. Playing with a mind reader is tough and she isn't a skilled Mey Wong player. She passes for a professional amateur at everything from sex

to smuggling, but at her core she's a player, indeed. The galaxy's her game. She'll win tonight no matter what. There are only two outcomes she accepts anymore: win and win. Truth be told she can't decide which kind of win she'll enjoy more with this wager. There's something alluring about his tentacles. She'd probably enjoy him despite the apparent coolness of his features.

"I'm going to hold you down while you squirm," he says.

"Cocky much?" Jupiter asks with a smirk. He's a master Mey Wong player. His intellect, his smirk and his physicality turn her on. There are just so many potential points of contact and, my God, there couldn't be a more flexible lover in the galaxy. There isn't a direction he couldn't move. An image flashes through her mind. She's in a large zero-gravity chamber, his embrace the only anchor. Her vulnerable and naked, hair a mess floating about her like she's Medusa. His tentacles, his whim, are all that keep her from being stranded in weightless space, drifting indefinitely. She shakes the chills from her body and forces her pupils to the board. Her panties are damp.

"I'm enjoying your thoughts," he says with a leer.

"Are you trying to goad me into a mental defense?" Jupiter asks, ignoring the blush rising to her cheeks.

"I am curious. For those not used to the Xoidai, defensive fear is normal."

"With a face like mine, it's always been impossible to hide thoughts or feelings, so I don't try. I don't play poker. And I don't lie." Since he has no visible mouth, Jupiter isn't sure how she knows he's smiling at her response, but there's something in the quality of his person that has the glow of a smile.

"Astral check."

Lord Vollner enjoys saying that. She knows it as clearly as she *hears the words in her mind. It isn't a surprise that he's won.*

It isn't a surprise that she's enjoying his rewards. But it is surprising how quickly she's found herself naked and strapped to the wall. And at the complete lack of sting in losing the game. She's never been so graced with good gamesmanship.

"Strapped" maybe wasn't the right word. It's tentacles, not straps, holding her limbs apart and pinning them to the wall. The metal walls are cool on her back and shockingly erotic. Rather than hard, they feel firm and empty, ready to be filled, just like she is.

She tests his grip with a thrust of her arm. His tentacles are as strong as steel. Damn, his flexibility is matched so perfectly with strength. He's all muscle. Fuck. Lucky bitch, the universe is full of bonuses with her name written all over them. A suction cup latches on just below her left nipple.

"Your thoughts are the most delightful mix of lust and wonder," he says.

Another suction cup latches on a half inch from the first. One sucking cup at a time, Lord Vollner surrounds her areola. Then he does the most delightful roiling pattern of pushing and pulling around her lone exposed nipple. It's a delicious outrage. That nipple is screaming, "Me! Suck me!"

Whack! A tentacle lashes her exposed and wanting nipple.

She groans and her self-possession drains away. She thought she'd already surrendered, but apparently she'd been holding out. Now it's his tentacles and nothing else. She's limp with ecstasy.

Her legs spread wider. Oh God, his tentacle is caressing her ass. While her pussy hangs wide open to the empty room. The beautiful bastard. Her thighs tense and immediately release. Ass play is not wise to struggle against. She wants the pleasure, but her poor neglected pussy protests its abandonment, so cruelly displayed. The fucking mind reader knows she likes it in the ass, and he knows exactly why she's scared. She trembles at the pain that could come any moment. She tries to speak.

"I...a..."

A tentacle winds into her mouth, caressing her tongue. She moans. The tentacle at her ass squirms about. It almost tickles. She half tries to say so.

How could this feel so good? Does he have drugs in his tentacles?

A suction cup latches on to her clit. Her body bucks and she screams. She isn't sure if it's pleasure, frustration or the edge of too much. The suction's intense. Way fucking intense, but the more she screams the more his tentacle slides into her mouth.

She's pinned at the ankles and wrists to a cold metal wall. Her clit and breasts suctioned and tentacles in her ass and mouth. She's never been happier. And yet, she thinks, she'll go mad if she doesn't get something shoved in her pu—

Fuck! It's like he can read her mind, because he fucking can. She would giggle but this is no time for giggles. Drool runs down her chin and onto her heaving breasts. The tentacle in her ass pulls out as the one in her mouth delves impossibly deep down her throat, and then the tide reverses. The tentacle in her mouth pulls out. She doesn't want it to go. She shakes her head no. It slides out and the tentacle in her ass goes in. So deep. Her eyes tear up. There's just enough tentacle in her mouth that she can't speak. She knows he can hear her thoughts, but she isn't sure which thoughts she's chosen as hers unless she says them out loud.

FUCK.

He plunges another tentacle into her pussy. She's so lost in the push and pull she can't tell what's coming and going. Vollner withdraws the tentacle from her mouth. It winds around her neck and slaps her. She opens wide. He drives that tentacle back in her mouth, fat and wide this time, like he wants to see how wide she can take it. The tentacle around her neck tightens and pulls. Fuck, fuck, fuck, fuck, fuck. What the hell. Leverage. All he needs is some leverage. He slides the suction cup up her clit while penetrating her with the lower of his extremities. Her eyes roll back in her head.

"You are a goddess," he says.

She explodes in orgasm. Her eyes pop open with the force of the convulsions and she screams despite the tentacle in her mouth.

She shakes and quivers.

When had the hard press of tentacles become a soft bed entwined about her?

"Thank you," she says.

"Thank you," says Lord Vollner, laughing.

I'm happy with my masturbation session. I've got footage, and I'm basking in the afterglow of an orgasm. I want to roll over and go back to sleep. That's what I don't like about sex in the morning; it always makes me want to sleep the rest of the day away.

I'm happy with my footage but as I edit I see a problem. Just as my moans sink to that primal place, a vaginal boogie pops into view, front and center. Cringe. Honest depictions of sexuality are one thing, vaginal boogies are another.

I was not going to post my boogie footage online.

Unfortunately the offending boogie appears just before I orgasm and is impossible to crop from the frame. I scold myself for not checking my pussy before the shoot and sprucing it up down there, prior to pointing a camera at it.

I often justify shooting without primping first as a way of

being genuine, but now it just seems lazy and ill considered. Watching the footage I can't see anything else but that little globular boogie migrating across labial folds as my fingers work in furious circles.

Damn it. It's a distraction from sexy noises, jiggling breasts and wanting holes.

I hate you, evil little vaginal boogie! How dare you embarrass me?

I sit and pout. I make a futile attempt to crop it out.

I discover that it is indeed as futile as I thought it would be. This is so frustrating. You wake up early, you masturbate at an inconvenient time of day so you can meet your deadlines and then at the climactic moment, it's shit. Or boogies. I'm glad it's not literally shit. I've never had a urinary tract infection and I'd like to keep it that way. Boogies are way better than shit. But they still aren't good.

How can I fix this? Or at least make it workable?

I blow my lips like a horse. Maybe I'm bored of being stuck in the stables. I'm stalling. My mind wanders into daydreams, and I end up back in space with Lord Vollner. What other ways could he make me come? Can you imagine an eight-legged lover in an orgy, or at least a threesome? My body pressed to another woman's, both of us impaled on the same male members. Good God. The possibilities. Theoretically you could aim for an eight-way orgasm, how cool would that be?

I'm crazy, a simultaneous orgasm between two people can be challenging enough.

But, in space, with a mind reader for a lover, anything is possible, right?

A girl can dream.

Hey, wait. In space. In space, anything is possible. I'm not sure that's really a true statement. But whatever, somewhere in the editing software I saw a visual filter that looked alien. I can set this video in space. I can edit in the actual fantasy I was having while I filmed.

Fuck. I think it will work. I think it will really, really work. It might even be better than it would have been before.

Until this moment I'd not intended to even allude to what I'd been imagining while I masturbated. The audience would enjoy the sight of my gyrating wet pussy, so it hadn't occurred to me to let them in on the contents of my mind. I hadn't talked about my fantasies as I filmed. I wasn't thinking about them as I edited. I'd been thinking in terms of showing the physical manipulation and simple sensuality of me in bed with my fingers. Geez, what an almost-missed opportunity. Crikey, alien sex is so much more exciting.

Can you believe that without that one little vagina boogie, I'd have left all of that intergalactic sexual fantasy out? I wouldn't have even hinted at it. Sometimes I'm an idiot. Good thing I have a higher power looking out for me, or maybe a lower power in this case. Whether it's astral guidance or God in drag, in this moment I am deeply and profoundly thankful to all my vaginal secretions. Thank you, little boogie, for showing me the way. This video wouldn't be half as awesome without you.

Sex with Aliens is an essay inspired by filming and editing *Alien Sex*, January 2016.

9

v-day

AFTER A FEW MONTHS of sexy-time dates with myself, I am bored. Horror of horrors, my budding relationship with me is growing routine—lie down, spread legs, get off. I am giving myself the masturbational equivalent of a quickie and I don't like it.

"You treat me no better than a guy would," I say to myself. "You should have higher standards. I'm astonished. You're as bad as anyone you've ever dated."

That's a nasty scolding to get from oneself. I shut my mouth, blush in shame and think about it. It was Valentine's Day, the day when all the unloved get to feel extra-excluded and neglected. It's the worst motherfucking holiday ever invented.

"Hey, me, you don't get to pitch a fit about being single on Valentine's Day. You chose to be without a relationship this year."

Yeah, but I can still hate it.

"Or you can be true to the intention behind your masturbation practice and explore what your resistance is about instead."

You sound like a dork, you pretentious self-help–loving retard.

"I love you."

I know, I say to myself with an eye roll, but some part of me is secretly grateful.

With a bit of a peevish taint to my demeanor, I set out to treat myself special. I'm stumped. How on earth do I go about romancing myself?

The question is so stupid, so humiliating, it's like I'm staring at a concrete wall waiting for my turn at the institution. I wonder how long this will take. I wonder if it will work. I wonder why I'm even here trying. Through all the angst, the wall stays blank, ugly and cold.

Since I have no fucking clue how someone treats themselves well, I'm going to pretend I'm someone else. Where would I start if I were romancing a woman? Where would I start if I were writing the script for a new boyfriend to romance me? I don't know. I don't have any experience with this kind of shit. I've always dated tough guys who don't cater to whims or weakness.

Fuck. This is hard.

I give up. If I were writing a romantic script, I'd just have to go with Valentine clichés because I have no idea what I really want. Chocolates, jewelry, bubble bath, music, flowers, massage…none of it excites me, but I don't have any better ideas.

I take a breath. I am going to make this Valentine's Day special, and I'm going to masturbate. I'm going to treat me the way I'd want to be treated by someone else. I look around the house for inspiration. If I had a few hundred dollars I'd probably order chocolates delivered or something, but I'm broke. A bouquet of half-wilted flowers sits on the counter. *It's time to throw them out,* I think.

Just before my fingers open to let the stems drop into the garbage pail, I'm inspired. I grab a bowl from the cupboard and pluck the petals. I'll repurpose these flowers for my masturbation video. I separate roses, carnations and baby's breath into soft piles of potential. Then further separate the carnation petals from their stems. The rest I leave whole.

I make my bed, put the camera on slow motion and sprinkle pink carnation petals on the slate-colored sheets. In slow motion, the petals will land on the bed with solemn gravity. The shift in time turns soft petals into heavy thudding things. I like that. I finish scattering them loosely about the bed. I wish I had another bowl or two. They're like velvet between my fingertips, but there's enough. The carnation petals are prettier and less cheesy than I imagined. It's a bed fit for a tasteful princess. After my bath, it'll be ready and waiting for me. I like that.

The roses look lovely on the windowsill next to the tub, fat globs of fading beauty in the soft light, their pink petals laced with just a bit of shriveled brown. I should start my bath but I hesitate. I light a small candle for the far edge of the tub. The bathroom is a tight obstacle course with two tripods wedged between the tub and toilet. I should run my bath. I don't want to. Am I stalling or is this just part of the creative process?

I'm not sure, but I decide I need some sparkle. It doesn't take much pilfering about in the craft closet before I procure the perfect vial of glitter. This Valentine's Day will shine, literally if not emotionally. I'm pleased with myself; I've never heard of anyone else taking a glitter bath. I'm super original and creative. I hope I don't fuck up the drain mechanism or clog the pipe.

My bathtub is beautiful 1920s porcelain. Separate hot and cold knobs. I fiddle for the right mix as water gushes out with eager force. Glitter cascades into the water in a shimmer of red. I'm mesmerized by the falling flecks of light. How can there be so much sparkle in such a small speck? A notion nibbles at me—baby's breath would be a lovely addition, red sparkle and delicate white blossoms.

When I can't justify any more diversions without suspecting myself of gross and blatant procrastination, I undress and hop in the tub.

Part of me wants to sit and stew in the glittery water looking miserable; self-love on Valentine's Day is embarrassing and pathetic. But I'm making a video of my masturbation practice, and those thoughts sound more like self-abuse than self-love. Instead, I act like I'm having fun. I swirl the glitter.

I splash.

I spit blossoms at the camera.

Coy flirtation with undercurrents of aggression. It's sexy.

Ten minutes later and I'm done with flirtations. It's time to get on with foreplay.

The glitter on my skin looks more like sand than sparkle, but I don't try to get it off. I pat gently and the towel takes the moisture. When I'm dry enough, I crawl into the flower petals on my bed. I massage myself, languid breast strokes and belly rubs. I squeeze my shoulders and press a few fingerfuls of coconut oil onto my labia.

With men, my favorite kind of foreplay has always been anticipation stoked by tease and denial. When a man touches me everywhere except my pussy, I think I'm dying from an agony of pleasure and want. I try to do the same for myself now. I tease. I can touch anywhere but between my legs.

Desire.

Appetite.

Sex hunger.

My breathing grows ragged and I succumb to a single touch.

Bad girl. I withdraw the errant finger. *Will, reassert yourself.* Thighs, butt, belly. I stroke and knead. I touch my plump belly and stretch marks without apology or hesitation. Fuck body issues. I'm in my body and it's glorious.

I'm ready for penetration. I've been ready forever.

I push my fingers in just a little. I pause and show the camera. My fingertips are gooey with pussy goodness. That was effective foreplay. I try not to get prideful. I rub and rub. It feels good but I'm not getting that edge-of-orgasm feeling. Nope, no edge in sight. Edge, oh edge, where are you?

I need something to push me over into mindless physicality, but first I have to find it.

The flower petals are soft. I like rubbing them on myself. They are softer even than my skin. The petals travel. They are going naughty places. Delicately, I circle my anus with a petal, around and around. My ass is oh, so full of nerve endings.

I have an idea.

I should be double stuffed with petals. Call me a Valentine Oreo. I push the petals in just enough to stick. I have a soft pink protrusion from my ass, half-in, half-out. I feel anointed. My ass was built for flower petals. I hurriedly poke a few petals in my pussy as I feel the orgasm building, I don't have much ti—

Fuck.

Orgasm.

I'm a cornucopia of pleasure, with petals pouring forth in apt abundance.

I am shining from more than just the glitter.

Usually I'd be done, but this is Valentine's Day and I am special. I want to be romanced big once in a while. I wish I didn't have to do it myself, but I'm being a big girl. The thought makes me sad. But even in the sadness there is pleasure. I think of getting out of bed, cleaning up and washing off. Ugh. I went to a lot of fuss to set all this up; I should enjoy it longer.

I press on for a second orgasm.

I shove a thicker wad of flower petals in my ass and film a little more. Asshole, butt cheeks, legs and feet. Whoa, my pussy clenches in a flutter of hot tight pulses.

That second orgasm came too easy. But it was little.

I keep at it.

Could there be three?

That would be unprecedented. I was always a one-and-done girl, until my last lover gave me five orgasms our very first time together. But that was all him, right?

I couldn't give myself three orgasms in a row, could I?

Me, the glitter and the soft fine flowers are going for a triple score. I'm all about the petal play, or the floral anal pleasure. Should something that smells so sweet be shoved up my ass?

Definitely.

And maybe something else too. I put a finger up my ass.

Oh, oh, oh, oh, yes.

Bad, bad girl.

A bubble of amazing energy bursts from my middle, big and wet. The undissipated energy runs to the end of my limbs and frizzles like pop rocks.

I lie there and giggle.

That was so fucking worth it.

Happy Valentine's Day, me.

V-Day is an essay inspired by filming and editing *Valentine Madness: Parts I, II & III*, February 2016.

9 ¾

the ugly flowers

THE DOORBELL RINGS. My body reacts like someone jumped out of the bushes at me. Awake and wary, I head for the door. A delivery man stands there with flowers. Adrenaline turns into excited curiosity as the flowers pass from his hands to mine. I can't imagine who would send me flowers, or why. Is it my ex-lover just saying he's thinking of me? Is it a new admirer? Maybe it's that friend with benefits I haven't seen in a while? That would be nice. As soon as the flowers are on the table and my hands are free, I grab the little card and read the greeting. My heart sinks.

They are from my brother.

I'm so disappointed.

Worse.

Not only am I crushed that they're just from my little brother, I also know how small that ingratitude makes me.

I scold myself.

My brother knows I'm in a hard place. He knows it sucks that the legal aspects of my divorce are dragging on forever. Out of the blue he sends his love and support via flowers.

What kind of fuckturd sister is utterly disappointed by that?

He's being a good brother. A really good brother, and I should appreciate it. He went through his divorce first and he's sending a little torch of encouragement, a "you can do it" message. He knows how hard it is. He deserves a Purple Heart for sending flowers, but all I feel is grudging resentment.

I tell my mind to be nice, and then I spend the next few weeks hating these flowers. I'm angry every time I see them. They're not a beautiful bouquet, they're an ugly lump of carnations with a few scattered roses, probably just so they could justify overcharging for it. I hate carnations.

I try not to look at the flowers because all I see is what my lover never sent me. I know it's miserly to go from good cheer to foulness because they aren't from a lover. It shouldn't matter, but it does. That's how it is. We want the love we want. Being offered other love isn't a consolation. It just isn't. I'm more miserable for having gotten flowers from my little brother than if I'd gotten nothing at all. I've never appreciated irony less.

By Valentine's Day the roses are starting to droop. I'm glad I can finally throw the whole damn thing away. Just before my fingers open to let the stems drop into the garbage, though, I'm inspired.

I can use these. I can use them in my film. Flower petals on a bed is a traditional romantic gesture, or a Hollywood one. Visual interest is good, variety is good. I don't want to make the same old damn Masturbation Monday video every week.

I grab the scissors from the counter behind me. As carnation petals fall, I see so much more to them than there seemed. Like a dress unpleated at the waist, petals triple in volume when freed from their stems. The bowl fills fast. I had no idea there was so much pink velvet hidden in each trite little flower. Separated from their stems, they're the most beautiful petals I've ever seen.

the ugly flowers

And the softest. I can't stop rubbing them between my fingers.

It is an absolute joy to throw the petals onto my blue-gray sheets. I head back to the bouquet to see what other beauty I can find there.

The roses want to float in bowls of water by my bath. They said so. I happily lop their heads off and flounce into the bathroom to place them lovingly on the windowsill. Ohhh, and there is baby's breath! What a romantic name for a flower. I have to find something to do with the baby's breath. I gather the delicate lace of stems and buds from the bouquet until all that's left is the greenery. I remember hunting salal in the woods with my father when I was young; we sold it to floral shops. They used it for greenery in bouquets like this. It was one of my father's many short-lived money-making schemes. I drop the greenery into the bin and let it go.

By the end of the filming I'm enraptured by these flowers. I can honestly say I've never appreciated or enjoyed a bouquet of flowers more thoroughly than I have this one.

And some time later I realized that I had not just used flowers from my brother in a sex video, but I'd shoved them up my ass. I am mortified. Who the fuck has to shove the petals up their ass before they can truly appreciate being sent flowers?

I am in awe of, and chagrined by, the innocence of my perversions.

And, umm, one more thing, Dear Reader. If you know my brother, ask him about the weather. Ask him about his beautiful children and lovely wife. Ask about his mountain bike. Tell him to say hi to his sister for you. Just don't tell him about this chapter.

He really doesn't need to know.

The Ugly Flowers is an essay inspired by filming and editing *Valentine Madness: Parts I, II & III*, February 2016.

10

moon boobs

I DON'T WANT to masturbate.

"Do it anyway," I tell myself.

If anyone else told me that they didn't want to masturbate, I'd say, "Sexual agendas are no good. Listen to yourself. Masturbate only when you feel like it." But there is more than one me, and an earlier me made a commitment to finding more room in her life for joy and pleasure. That me made a commitment to a practice and a practice takes discipline, even if you're feeling about as sexy as a flat tire. Martial arts and meditation practices aren't for when you already feel strong or calm. They're intended to cultivate strength and calm so that you may command them when needed.

This is the lecture I give myself as I set about my masturbation practice with about as much enthusiasm as I'd have for fixing said flat tire in the rain. I point the camera at myself and hope to find something beautiful and compelling. An image worth sharing.

I lie on my back in bed, breasts bare. I rub my clit for all it's worth, because damn it, when *am* I going to feel sexy? Divorce isn't sexy. Being alone, hurt and almost forty isn't sexy. Being me isn't sexy—unless I choose to make it so.

I look at the camera, and the image reflected back at me. I look stupid. I adjust the camera, reposition myself and check again. It's worse. I move the entire tripod to the other side of my bed and crank the handle for more height.

Camera adjustments are part of the process. I always do them until I find a decent angle. I usually find something pleasing. It isn't hard. My breasts are curvy and curves are beautiful. I quest after the perfect angle from which to capture these curvy wurvies. A little to the left. Ugh, the boobs look floppy. I rotate the camera a bit farther. Crap on toast, did I age significantly since pointing the camera at myself last week? My boobs are deflated sacks of lameness. I prop myself on pillows. Grrr. I tilt my torso to the side. No. I move the camera, just one more try. And another. Each adjustment yields more displeasure. I want to hurl the tripod across the room, but it's my favorite tripod.

The world is wrong and unfair. Boobs are supposed to be pliant and comforting, not unphotogenic, disagreeable obstinate lumps.

Right now, it's me vs. my boobs. And I think I'm losing.

Usually I pride myself on not resting until I feel lady luck beside me in all my creative pursuits. When she's there I'm certain of the win; it's exhilarating. Each time I move the camera I wait for her whisper, but it's like my fucking ears are clogged.

The progression of increasingly terrible angles is infuriating. I look less attractive now than when I started. I yield. Fuck it. I will document the imperfection of it all, the imperfection of me. Documenting actual masturbation is the goal. Apparently that includes this unsexy, frustrated, spitting-annoyed woman called "me."

I'm grumpy, my hair is dumb, my boobs are dumb and there's a pimple on my ass. I should probably crawl under a rock and die. But I don't have a rock big enough. And I'd probably get cold. Actually that sounds really uncomfortable, and full of spiders. Never mind.

"Back up, get some perspective, me." In general I can ignore, mitigate or dive in when confronted with things I do not like. The ass pimple I'd ignore if it weren't a particularly atrocious one. But it is, and that's why I'm masturbating with the camera from a front angle and wearing lacy underoos that cover my butt cheeks. I'm not trying to be fake. I don't like looking at ass pimples. And this is about what turns me on.

Let's call this "Strategy P," for focusing on the positive. Like all strategies, it's great unless it's not working. Right now, it is totally not working. If focusing on the positive isn't enough, I explore the negative. Theoretically, I might pop the pimple on camera. But let's be real, pimples are never ready to pop when you want them to be. And, except for people with a pimple-popping fetish, that would be gross in a bad way. I am kinda fascinated by popping pimples, but not sexually excited by it. This is getting weird.

Maybe a better example is feeling fat. I might grab said fat. I might jiggle it, wiggle it and eventually get bored or distracted. For functional purposes here, boredom and distraction in the face of what once was utterly distressing, like fatness, is a functionally reasonable definition of self-acceptance as far as I'm concerned. In the aftermath of accepting the fat, something else emerges. That something else is grounded, real and immediate.

It's alive. It's connected. Let's call this "Strategy E," for em-fucking-brace it.

Since today "Strategy P" failed, I limply wiggle my boobs in an attempt at "Strategy E." But I cannot embrace them. They are flat like pressed flowers yet oddly wrinkled. I hate them. They look decades older than me, like someone trying to make prunes out of peaches. It's not fair. I've seen women in their seventies with perkier tits.

I am body positive. Therefore I should feel good about my body, unconditionally.

But I don't.

I could try, but I'd be faking it. And that's worse. It's impotent thinking, and numb denial. It's hoping that if you wish harder you'll stop feeling like you've failed yourself. It's a double layer of self-alienation.

Should, should, should.

I should be in a sexy mood. My camera angle should be flattering. My boobs should look rounder. I shouldn't have to try. And I should shut the fuck up.

My boob dissatisfaction is alienating. Alienation. Self-alienation. Alienated from the self.

Aliens. What if my boobs were aliens? Or the eggs of aliens, waiting to hatch open. Jesus Fucking Christ, that's creepy. Yuck.

Nice thoughts, come here, nice thoughts. Come on. Think of my boobs not as aliens but maybe appreciated by aliens. Envision a happy and safe intergalactic me, being a super sexy space slut.

Huh, I wonder how my boobs would act in zero gravity. Or low gravity. Imagine how fabulously perky my boobs would be on the moon. Picture it, me taking Armstrong's epic jumps, the long arc and slow descent, with me naked except for my space helmet. My boobs would bounce gloriously up, as if in slo-mo, reverberating and quivering in flotatious wonder.

If I stood still, would they kind of hover at my chest?

These ponderings leave me feeling less annoyed, but I'm still a long leap from sexy.

I keep my fingers at my clit, trying to work myself into a state. I rub and rub and rub. But I am not going to come. Maybe I should call them "chest orbs" instead of "boobs." Maybe "boobs" just isn't a sexy word.

Orbs, chest orbs. Nah, "orbs" isn't a sexier word.

I don't know what is sexy.

I just don't know.

I guess I could ask.

"Hey me," I say, "what would turn you on?"

Nipple clamps.

Huh, that totally hadn't occurred to me, but it absolutely fits. Proper punishment for wayward tits. I pop out of bed and rummage around in the bottom of the suitcase in my closet. I'm keenly aware of my bare ass pointing out at the empty room. I feel exposed though I'm alone. Oh no, I can't find the nipple clamps. *Not optional,* I tell myself. I need those clamps! My fingers fumble along, groping. *Use the Force,* I tell them, *find the clamps.* More scrambling, more searching…I've got them! The cold weighty steel chain hangs from my fingers. It's beautiful.

Thin pincer clamps dangle at each end. The swinging chain from my tits will look so good on film, or at least intriguing. I smile. These clamps look like tweezers with an extra-long neck, like a giraffe. Black plastic nubs cover the pincer ends. I place my left nipple between the shiny black pincers. My tongue pokes out of my lips as I concentrate on attaching it to myself. It's a bit of a strain to see my nipple. When I look down it's only like six inches from my face. I push the thought of needing reading glasses from my mind; I am too young for that shit. I slide the O-ring along the metal shaft until it hurts just a little, in a good way. I let go. It holds, yay!

The right nipple slips out from between the pincers as I tighten. I try again. And again. Finally, the chain hangs down, cold on my bare belly. I don't care if it pulls my saggy boobs lower, the pressure feels good. I've only used these clamps once or twice before. I bought them for my first lover, after my marriage became an open marriage. He loved having his nipples pinched hard, but I discovered that nipple clamps did wonders for me too. The pain clears my mind of doubt. I am all here, right now.

It's a more intense sensation than pain. It pulls me out of my head and into my body. I lie down and pull the chain upward. The delicate skin of my tiny nipples stretches into odd triangles. I turn over. When I'm on all fours the camera sees the delightful pull of the chain between the two clamps as it settles into a fine inverted arch. I jiggle and watch the chain swing. It's shiny.

I tug gently to increase the intensity. A clamp slips.

Blarg. Today, even nipple clamps won't subdue my unruly boobs. That's how disagreeable they are. God fucking damn it.

Out of the murky morass of miserable unsexiness an idea springs forth. Nipple clamps could pinch other places too. Down-low places. Labial places. Mwahaha. Given a proper dose of frustration, and time to ferment, the murk spits out a solution.

I smile at the camera and remove the remaining nipple

clamp suggestively, one eyebrow raised. I drag the chain down my belly. And tickle myself through my panties.

Bye, bye, panties.

Slick membranous folds slip between my fingers. Will nipple clamps even attach with so much wetness? I'm scared the clamps will hurt more on these delicate folds than they did on my nipples. Tenderly, I tighten the pincers. I tug the chain ever so lightly. It holds. I lean back, smiling broader. The chain drapes around my pussy, pulling my labia apart. It is heavy, and cold. Glorious girl juice flows freely. The nipple clamps slip off. I don't begrudge them. I just reattach them. I'm happy.

Warm energy builds. I can tell an orgasm is coming, as long as I don't overthink it. I swirl the chain. It circles, up, down and all around, pulling my pussy gently this way and that. I look at myself. I am red and swollen and so slick.

Yes, the orgasm is coming.

Whamo bamo, I'm convulsing in joy.

I pause and feel the satisfaction of the moment.

All that time and frustration, and then when it finally comes the ball of orgasmic pleasure slips into the world as if it was always right there waiting for me.

Rascally bastard.

Moon Boobs is an essay inspired by filming and editing *Moon Boobs*, March 2016.

11

purple penis eater

I FLIP THE TOP OPEN on the old blue suitcase in the back of my closet. Its red trim is monogrammed with Nana's initials in gold. The chunky brass buckle and still-smooth zipper are admirable in their craftsmanship. Like everything about Nana, it's strikingly fashionable. Nana was a poster child for that 1950s veneer of perfection, her sophisticated tastes hiding all the deep dark secrets.

I keep my sex toys in it. It sounds romantic, but it's surprisingly inconvenient, I realize as I try to find my butt plug. I want it for this masturbation shoot. I rummage about in the overflow of whackers, ticklers and God knows what. No matter how I scootch the contents about, I cannot find the stinking butt plug. I don't want candles, ribbons or nipple clamps. I want my small black-silicone, curved-flange, conical thingy widget for rear-end insertion.

No luck.

Instead I come up with two purple strap-ons and a metallic cock-sized vibrator, also purple. I'm disappointed about the butt plug but willing to roll with the punches. Finding a fistful of suitable second-choice sex toys leaves me feeling like life is not that bad.

I shut the door to my bedroom with my foot. I have three dildos in my hands and no intention of coming out until I've procured a significant amount of physical pleasure. I'm a bit in awe of myself. I have grown into a gloriously hedonistic person. I feel vaguely sorry for that girl who felt gross and guilty about touching herself. I know she turned into me eventually so I don't feel too sorry for her. She had to learn what she had to learn. I'm here now, I remind myself, and so ready to celebrate my accomplishments.

With only two hands it could be a challenge to employ three dildos at once. Lucky for me, one is a strap-on. It's the first strap-on I ever bought and is still my favorite despite its diminutive stature. It may be a small penis but I get a huge girl boner putting it on. I step into the harness and tug it tight.

Strapping a penis to my pelvis is a relatively new experience. It's mesmerizing. It pokes out into the world ahead of me. I love its eager sproingy bounce. It just begs to be thrust into things. It's hard to behave with a phallus leading the way. I muse at how difficult it must be for men to deal with such an exuberant protuberance actually hardwired to their brains.

I stroke my little cock in much the same manner and rhythm as my high school not-boyfriend did, quick and heavy on the downstroke. Pete's dick was a hell of a lot thicker, but mine is purple and belongs to me. I'm probably a bit too happy about this constructed cock attached to my body. My inner voice sounds drunk with power as it gleefully repeats one word, "mine," "mine," "mine"! That thought ends with a maniacal laugh reel.

purple penis eater

The back side of the strap-on frames my ass with inch-wide black nylon strips of badassness. They keep that cock secured nice and snug. The straps wrap around each thigh, holding the mounting pad atop my mound. It produces a soft, alluring pressure, urging me to do something naughty.

The nylon straps run parallel to the lace of my thigh highs, two black stripes just below my extremely fair bare ass. Besides the thigh highs and strap-on, I'm naked. My large round breasts have nipples as diminutive as my cock. My itty-bitty pieces feel perfectly sized and mega magnetic.

I've always thought of myself as the antithesis of exotic. I look like the quintessential American girl next door, stuffed on apple pie and white bread, except my mom actually raised me on lentil soup and bean burritos. But you get the point. I think of myself as pretty, in a boring ordinary way.

A pair of thigh highs and a strap-on turn this good girl next door into something unexpected. Something dangerous. I'm tinged with threat. Latent aggression suffuses my soul with the possibility of penetration. My new protuberance poses so many potentialities. It's an itty-bitty threat. It's also perky, purple and slender; these aspects match my soft cuddly innocence. All the better to camouflage newer, more unsettling urges.

There's something exciting about the threat of power for both the wielder and the potential submissive. Anyone watching my video might start imagining what it'd be like to have me thrusting deep inside them. I stroke my little cock. I love it. I'm surprised at how good it feels. The rhythmic pressure on my mound radiates warmth. The slick cylinder in my palm is so solid, so there. The lube makes a sloppy sound every time I whack down. It's so naughty.

I'm self-satisfied to the point of gloating.

But I have three phallic toys to employ today. One down, two to go.

The next is the purple metal one. It vibrates if you press the little button. I don't press it. One sensation at a time. The smooth metal against my labia is cool. I ignore the trickle of blood between my legs. Menstruation holds no eroticism for me. I rarely even masturbate while on my period. I usually get horny as fuck in the days leading up to it, but only on rare occasions have I rubbed one out on my period. When I do, I touch myself through my menstrual pad. Masturbation during menstruation is meh, at best. Disgusting at worst.

For the most part I do a remarkable job of timing it so weekly filming sessions just happened to miss my bloody days. But this time I didn't manage it. I push the shiny purple thing in deep. It hides the blood. The smooth metal warms fast. Its length fills me. I can't help but wiggle my hips. I clamp my legs together. This smooth dildo will get away from me if I'm not careful. It has a habit of shooting out.

I place the third penile object in my mouth with a flirtatious glance at the camera. My spit makes it shine. I imagine the audience wishing their cocks were in my mouth, wishing it so bad. I must be quite a pretty picture in fishnets, wearing one dildo, having another up my crotch and a third in my mouth.

I don't actually like the third purple dildo. I bought it as an upgrade strap-on for my harness. It's a more realistic penis size but not a realistic shape. It's bulbous on the end and too slender through the shaft. It was an experimental purchase, and some experiments fail. But I'm too frugal to throw it away.

Without the butt plug, I'm just doing oral and vaginal

insertions while stroking the strap-on, but I can't get butt play off my mind. The urge has grown, not subsided. I contemplate this bulbous-ended dildo going in my ass. It seems impossible. The plug starts small, and never gets as big as the bulbous part at the beginning of this one. I draw comfort from the dildo, still in my mouth. I was a tenacious thumb sucker. Oral fixations may morph, but they never entirely disappear.

I close my eyes and imagine my old lover's cock in my mouth. We hadn't spoken from August until December. Then I emailed him, just a note to tell him I was thinking of him. That led to a hookup or two, but other than that it's been emails only. It isn't cheating. I only promised myself no *new* relationships.

I've missed him so much.

I want to wrap all my limbs around him. He's the kind of lover who gives black men a reputation as inexhaustible. I want him everywhere and in every way, all at once. It's silly idealism, but I want to be his in every way. He's had my throat, all the way. He's been buried deep inside my pussy as far as he could go, but we didn't manage anal. We tried once. His cock isn't the hugest in the world, but it sure the fuck felt like it when he tried to stick me in the ass. It was the first and last time he tried. He took his go at my ass with little preamble. I screamed like a stuck pig and started hyperventilating.

I never hyperventilate.

This incident is one of the most embarrassing sexual stories of my life, not because it sounds terrible when I tell someone else, but because it feels terrible when I think of it. I wanted to be triumphant, I wanted it so bad. And I should have been able to take it. Really, truly, I am a badass. I can take almost anything. I gave birth without drugs, au naturel. My pain tolerance is high.

I don't know what happened. The hyperventilation could have been allergies. I was tied up in the basement and I'm sensitive to mold. It's not a reasonable excuse that I really want.

I just want another try, and I'm afraid he'll never give it to me. That's why I was looking for the butt plug. I want to show him I'm serious about ass play. I want to prove that I really, really can take it. If I prove that I can get a cock-sized object up my ass, maybe he'll try again. I'm not an ass virgin. I know part of the problem was the total lack of lube. And that he also went too fast. I want to show him how it looks when I go slow and steady.

Maybe not finding the butt plug is a blessing in disguise. A demonstration with something larger and more penis shaped could be more convincing, and he needs convincing. The almost-passing-out thing scared him off my ass altogether. He's been nowhere near it, even when I've asked.

Maybe he can learn from my masturbation video what he couldn't learn from me at the time. One, my body can take it. Two, slow and steady wins the race. Three, I really want it.

I want it, Daddy, I say to myself as I press the dildo tightly against my little sphincter. It's well lubed. I take a deep breath. This is hard and scary. The anal pressure is uncomfortable, and I'm afraid it's going to hurt any moment. I turn the vibrator on and pull it out of my vagina to get at my clit. Clitoral vibration is a welcome distraction from the anticipation of pain.

I close my eyes and see his beautiful face. I smile and nod eagerly.

"*My ass is yours,*" I say in my mind. My voice is gentle, calming and seductive.

He smiles back and presses the tip of his beautiful cock to my ass. He is radiant. We're radiant. I love him. I can't wait for him to be inside me. My quivery legs want to wrap around him.

The vibrator slides off my clit and I put it back. I sneeze and lose the half inch I'd gained on my ass. Blarg! Not fair! Anal ain't easy, especially if you sneeze.

Big breath. Concentrate. Focus. You will get this thing in your ass. You will show him it can be done. You'll show him you want it, and you want him. I close my eyes and imagine he's already seen the video, he's here now and he's fucking my ass.

"Daddy."

His naked body is beautiful to behold. I run my fingers across his cheek. "I love you."

The pressure at my ass is steady and intense. I imagine myself opening, but I feel closed as tight as a clam. Why is my ass so resistant?

"I submit to you, Daddy," I whisper. I would arch up and lick his ear but I'm afraid to move. I don't want to lose any gain, even if it's only been centimeters.

I keep the ass pressure steady and focus on my clit and the fantasy.

Daddy watches my face as he presses, slow and steady. He will have his way. He enjoys watching my submission unfold before him. He loves me. His hips push forward.

Pop. The fucking thing finally pops into my ass. Yay!

His gentle rhythmic hip thrusts are matched by his thumb on my clit.

"You like that?" he asks.

He knows the answer is yes, but he wants to hear me say it.

"Yes, Daddy. I love it."

Once it's in my ass, it's a wonder that it took so damn long to get there in the first place. I'm swept by the relief of success. It feels good. Triumph with an extra emphasis on *umph*. *Don't think too much,* I chastise myself. Just feel, and imagine.

Daddy is so happy inside me. Now that it's in, my fear is gone. I want him hard and fast.

"*Fuck me, Daddy. Please. My ass can take it. My ass wants it.*"

I wiggle into him and hold tight.

"*Fuck me, Daddy. Please.*"

He does.

The dildo slides in and out of my ass easily, the bulbous end an easy stopper making it worry free. It won't fall out accidentally. I won't have to start over. It's a hard reach, around my hip to my own ass. I'm enjoying the relative ease now that the difficult part is over. The vibrator is buzzing in my pussy, and there's a dildo up my ass. Life is good, and I sink back into daydreams.

Daddy's sweat drips on me. I love it. I would love to fuck him during one of his workouts. I love everything about him. His overdeveloped chest, his dark skin and the discipline it took to mold himself into the man that he is.

"*Fuck me, Daddy.*"

"*I love you,*" *he says.*

I can't say anything else. He's driving into me with ridiculous intensity but I'm not laughing. I can hardly speak.

His fingers wind tight in my hair. He's going to come in my ass. I know it a moment before he starts to groan. I feel his pleasure, and my own shoots through me.

My eyes roll and I orgasm, loud.

I catch my breath for a moment, resting in the afternoon sunlight, me and my three dildos.

Unfortunately, it's not over with the orgasm. It's over when the washing is done and everything is back in Nana's old suitcase. Three dirty dildos to wash; that's a happy hedonist. Okay, it's time to stop thinking about it and to actually disengage the bodily insertions. I wait. Maybe the dildos will self-eject. I wait longer. My body could push them out. I think it will. Won't it?

Doubt creeps in.

Yes!

The pussy vibrator self-ejects, just as I give up on it. But the dildo in the ass, that's not coming out on its own. Stupid bulbous end. This requires concentrated relaxing. I breathe slow. I force myself to stop making high short gaspy noises. Play it cool. You got this. I pull slowly, with one third of my strength. Once I hit the bulbous end, it stops moving. I keep a steady low pull on it, not too much. It moves so little I could be imagining it, but still it hurts.

Ow, ow, ow, ow, owie.

It's out. That's it.

And there, on its tip, is one perfect little crumb of poo.

Sexy.

Thanks, least-favorite ugly bulbous dildo, you were a useful pain in my ass.

Purple Penis Eater is an essay inspired by filming and editing *All My Dildos Are Purple*, March 2016.

12

birthday cock and ass love

I'VE BEEN TALKING TO MY "DADDY" almost every day but still haven't seen him again. It's weird. When we broke up, I replaced him with Instagram. Now that we're talking regularly again, I'm torn about who to say good morning to first. He wouldn't like that. He'd be offended that there was ever a shred of doubt as to whom I put first. With disdain for my fans, he's made it abundantly clear that he's not one of "them." I don't think he's seen the video I made with him in mind, the one I intended as an easy-to-swallow instruction manual for how he could fuck my ass successfully. I guess that also means he won't notice if I post good morning on Instagram before saying good morning to him. The disloyalty of this thought makes my heart hurt.

As my 39th birthday looms closer, I know two things. One, I really, really want to spend it with him. Two, he would ruin it. He hates birthdays. He doesn't even celebrate his own. I love birthdays and I have no intention of sacrificing mine on the altar of his hang-ups. Instead I ask myself a question.

"Hey me, what's the most wonderful thing we could possibly do for our birthday? What would be the most magnificent second-runner-up celebration?"

Obviously a hot air balloon ride would be the most amazing thing ever, duh. Haven't you been listening to yourself since you were like six years old?

A hot air balloon ride?!?! I am really impressed with how smart I am. That's some deep wisdom. I call two hot air balloon companies. The one I'm most comfortable with, because the pilot is a woman, is the first to call back. I ask if she'd be okay with me doing a nude photoshoot in front of the balloon as it fills in the early morning light. She says yes, and offers a photographer friend of hers as a second shooter, if I want one. I'm pretty sure she's a lesbian, but regardless of sexual orientation, I'm more comfortable getting naked in front of a woman I've never met before, than a man I've never met before. It's a likely bet that few hot air balloon pilots have had much experience working with nude models, and might bungle being respectful under the circumstances, but she sounds cool on the phone. I'm at ease, and excited.

I've been fascinated by hot air balloons since I was a child. One of my favorite library books, when my teeth were still deciduous, was about an Easter bunny Valentine's Day hot air balloon race. A few years ago, we lived in a house right under a semi-frequent ballooning path. We'd hear the gas burners while still in bed and run outside to watch them float by in the early morning light. One time, my daughter and I jumped on our bikes in our pajamas and followed them. We stayed a long time in the park where they landed, watching their beauty deflate.

I'm psyched. I've hyped myself into epic hot air balloon birthday excitement. I tell myself I'm all kinds of awesome if even my second-choice birthday plans are this badass. I'm super-duper cool. But I really wish I could spend my birthday in his arms. He's so indescribably beautiful. He's the most dominant man I've ever been with, a strict father, a demanding confidante. As a lover he's dynamic, both gentle and overwhelming in his physicality and strength. Sometimes he's an asshole, but he's the most beautiful asshole. His bossy demands make me feel wanted, and his large hands make me feel safe.

Ugh, I need more plans to fill the birthday void. I add a pedicure to the agenda, in the afternoon after the balloon ride. That should do it. I'll have the best birthday ever. Right?

Two days before my birthday the pilot tells me the weather isn't looking good. Even if it clears, the ground will still be too damp for ballooning. I try to look on the bright side. Maybe this is a sign. Maybe the balloon was just me settling for second best. Maybe I should have more faith that I can have what I really, really want. Maybe I should take a chance on him.

I want to.

I'm so nervous as I send him an email invitation to meet me on my birthday. The butterflies in my stomach are wingdinging about as I wait for his reply. To my utter shock and delight, he accepts.

I go to the mall in search of a dress with a 1950s-style skirt. A dress from the spanking fantasies I've had since meeting this beautiful man. I text him flirty pictures of me in half a dozen potential birthday dresses. His texts make me feel like a longed-for treat. We choose one dress together, and I buy another for good measure. A light blue one that would look just right on a hot air balloon ride, when the weather clears. Both dresses are perfect for an over-the-knee spanking from Daddy.

I bake a blackberry pie. Blackberries are the fruit of my

childhood and blackberry pie is the first thing I ever baked in my life. The crust was hard as a rock, and good for nothing but Frisbee practice, but the blackberry middle was divine. My blackberry pies are always divine. I want to share this piece of me with him. Pie is his favorite food. I mark the top in the shape of a wheat shaft. I'm no artist but it doesn't look bad. It's cute even, and it's going to be delicious. I put it in the oven for my baby and me.

It's my birthday, it's eleven in the morning and I'm confused. The pie is baked, the house is clean, lingerie is laid out and now I'm in the bath. But he hasn't mentioned when he's coming. He should be on his way by now considering the rest of his schedule today but he's made no indication that he's left home yet. We've texted and he's acting like it's any old day. I don't want to press him and ruin any kind of surprise. He's got kind of a short fuse sometimes.

The bath grows cold and I text him reluctantly.

I'm so sorry, he texts back. *I misunderstood. I feel terrible. I can't come today. I didn't think you meant today.*

Tomorrow? I ask.

Not tomorrow, he says. *But sometime.*

When?

I'll let you know when I can.

My heart drops, fast, long and hard. It's a squishy unrecognizable pile of gore when it finally lands with an irrevocable splat.

He isn't coming. He was never coming.

I look at the perfect pie I baked. I don't want to eat it, ever.

I cry instead of throwing the pie across the kitchen because I don't want to have to clean it up. Blackberries stain. I drive to my appointment, numb.

The pedicurist exfoliates my feet while tears stream down my face. This is the worst birthday ever. I knew he couldn't do a birthday and I tried anyway. I wanted it so bad. It's like I saw a hole of hurt and despair waiting for me. I knew it was there and I couldn't help falling in. I'm embarrassed by the tears but I can't hold them off. The torrential downpour from my face is at odds with the soothing spa music. My shell is being pampered, but I'm too withered in misery to soak anything in. Eventually the pedicurist asks about the tears. I tell her haltingly, in as few words as possible, what the scenario is. She nods her head. I feel remotely better.

There are still hours left in the day, and I have a life. I have commitments.

I buy a donut and head home to shoot a Masturbation Monday video for my 39th birthday. I'll make a farce of it. It's a Saturday and that's my ideal day for filming. Theoretically the rhythm goes, shoot Saturday, edit Sunday and post Monday. For my birthday I'm treating myself to timeliness with my schedule. That's a comforting thought.

Where my birthday celebration failed, routine picks up the pieces. I have a donut, a strap-on, a dildo and a nice shiny pair of black stilettos. The dildo has a suction cup on the bottom, something I'd never heard of until subscribing to some porn feeds on Twitter. That's some eye-popping madness. Usually I blush and hide my phone, but this was too intriguing. Using the close proximity to my birthday as an excuse, I ordered a suction-cup dildo for myself. It arrived a few days ago. I remove the packaging and gaze at it with indifference.

I am in no mood to rub out an orgasm. Being stood up on your birthday is the antithesis of an aphrodisiac. I don't try to

birthday cock and ass love

stimulate my clit; grief and rejection are too overwhelming. I start with a photo shoot. I've been working on a dick pic project. I strap on and pose with my faux dick nice and pert. Black straps, black stilettos, ample boobs and a surprise cock; these are things to distract even the most distraught mind. I start with my pink robe on, purple cock poking out. I throw up a heel and give some innocent faces to the camera. My mother always said if you're feeling depressed, stand up tall. There's something to that. Making faces as if I were happy, stretching my arms in invitation, crossing them with coyness, these poses lighten the shadows of my mood. I love still photography for the focus on the pose, one stance or one expression to speak for itself. It's different from video, where you actually can just speak, if you want to. Usually I don't. I like to leave my actions up for interpretation and debate; it makes me feel all artsy. By the end of my photoshoot my mood is sexable if not exactly sexy.

    I switch to video and try to eat a donut off my own dildo. I'm marginally successful. The cock is too big for the donut. I balance the broken halves and nibble at the confection between my legs. Awkward is sexy sometimes. I eat less than half the donut. It's all the birthday cake I'll have, and I won't touch that fucking pie. No. Don't go there. Sexy thoughts. How about my new suction-cup dildo? Put that baby on the floor and ride it hard.

    The suction cup doesn't stick to the hardwood floors with the tenacity I'd envisioned. I balance precariously and impale myself. I have to be exactly over the balance point or it comes loose. I fuck that cock and rub my clit for all I'm worth.

    Holy guacamole, total amazeballs, pleasure wells inside me. Pressure builds. Like a storm on the horizon, I know thunder is coming. I can feel the electricity.

I want the lightning.

I orgasm.

It's my birthday. Fuck him, I will come.

In the days that follow, he doesn't make time to see me. I decide no amount of apology excuses his continued absence. I stop talking to him. I stop giving him the opportunity to hurt me.

It was a shitty birthday, but don't feel sorry for me. Looking at the footage, I see a vulnerable awkwardness. I'm clumsy where in another mood I'd have been masterful, regardless of the stilettos. But the video is also endearing. I'd seen several women make videos with similar dildos, always in the bathroom for some odd reason. What fascinated me was the way their vaginas stretched and moved over the anchored dildos. It was different from handheld ones, or maybe the camera angle was different, coming from behind and below. One woman in particular had a trailing of thin skin sliding along the cock's shaft every time she disgorged it. I have no such mesmerizing membrane. The cock just plunged in and out of my hole with a happy bounce and a charming wobble. My lack of exotic excesses of vaginal skin is not a surprise, but still I'm a bit disappointed. I was hoping to discover something new and cool about my anatomy.

When comments on that video start rolling in they are overwhelmingly complimentary about one aspect in particular: my ass. Not the whole round derrière, but very specifically the anal sphincter bit. The electrical circuiting in my brain fizzled and popped. It was not previously in the realm of possibility that my anus could be complimented, let alone called beautiful. I've had anal sex a couple times but I just assumed my partners were in it for the taboo or the tightness, not that they actually found any beauty or poetry in that central point of my posterior.

In the days following my 39th birthday, I receive profuse love for a little bit of my anatomy that previously had been unquestioningly unlovable in my mind. Prior to that, I thought I'd pretty well accepted and appreciated my body. I wasn't even aware of the exceptions. I took my disdain for my anus as so natural that I wouldn't even have listed it on a list of things I didn't like about myself. I complain about my feet, my thighs and chin hairs, but at least they get attention. My poor ass was invisible and forgotten. That's the worst kind of neglect, utter and complete.

A huge thank-you, and a big birthday hug, to all those who offered kind words in response to my video and compliments for a hitherto unsung anus. It's enough to make me blush with pride. In the aftermath of a landslide of rectal praise, I see that it is indeed true.

I don't need a beautiful asshole; I have a beautiful asshole.

Birthday Cock and Ass Love is an essay inspired by filming and editing *Birthday Ride*, April 2016.

13

mile-high madness

I TRY NOT TO THINK about how dry the air is, or the germs circulating in the ventilation system. My breasts heave under the thin black crepe of my dress. No one around me seems alarmed by their monstrous enormity. I look down and double-check. My boobs do still fit in my bra despite everything about me suddenly feeling so ginormous, awkward and horny. Obviously my perception is off due to the smallness of the airplane, but that does nothing to alleviate how oversized I feel. I pretend to ignore the elbow that just brushed mine. Airplane rides are a jostle of accidental touches. I feel bound, tight and restricted.

It occurs to me how much like a BDSM scene this is. I am physically strapped down and waiting to be served. I've placed myself in the hands of the pilot and at the mercy of the stewardesses. They will be benevolent, if I am obedient. I must wait and be taken care of. I must be a good girl.

I'm in the middle seat with no window for distraction. The movie choices suck and I don't like their selection of music. I'm fidgety. I tuck a strand of hair behind my ear and glance down at my cleavage. There's nothing to take my mind from the inappropriate largeness of my breasts and the way they keep moving every time I breathe. How did I get so fucking turned on? I can't take four more hours of this. I look at my book. It's a romance. That's fuel I don't need right now. Restlessness gnaws at me. I'm hot between my legs.

I don't want to make a masturbation video on an airplane. The idea mortifies me more than most of my mortifying ideas. For someone as repressed as I've been, my predilection for masturbating on airplanes stands out. It's something I've done more than once, more than twice, more than three times. I do not want to fess up to that on camera. The urge to hide this part of myself makes it imperative that I don't. Why do I find it easier to confess new kinks and explorations than to document a longtime phenomenon? My goal isn't to paint a pretty picture but to document myself as I am, not as I think I should be. Airplanes have always made me horny. Damn it, I won't respect myself if I don't include a confession of my penchant for solo sky work.

With a sigh that looks like an epic heaving of the breasts, I latch the tray in the up position. Its thump reverberates through my thumb and forefinger. I lean forward to slip my mini tripod into my purse, breasts smooshing onto my knees. The pressure of sitting shifts from rump to pussy. Delightful. Naughty. Me.

The lap restraints on airplanes surpass all others. From cars to roller coasters, no other safety restraint I've submitted to even comes close. The quality, the click, the unapologetic strength and ease of adjustability, airplane seatbelts are the Rolls-Royce of restraints. My fingers fumble for the latch, and with the sexy whoosh of release I'm free. I'm also infinitesimally sad that the anticipation phase is almost over.

I signal to my neighbor that I have to get up. She scooches

back in her seat. I step over her, trying to keep my ass out of her face. Maybe I should have faced the other way, but then my tits would be in her face. Everything's so overstimulating and sexualized. I hope I'm not vibing unwanted sexual vibes at the people.

I gotta get to the bathroom.

Sexual frustration accumulates like static at ten thousand feet; it needs discharging. The narrowness of the aisle makes the sway of my hips feel twice as broad. Even strokes left and right as I try not to look too happy on my way to the cramped little naughty room. How many of the passengers watching me go down the long aisle guess that I'm going to the bathroom for recreational purposes? I've never wondered that of anyone else, and yet I'm sure they are all thinking it of me.

I'm lucky there aren't too many people on this flight. I wouldn't be able to hog the bathroom if I thought I was depriving anyone of needed access to the facilities. Thank goodness for vacancy signs and empty seats. I think of dirty diapers, diarrhea and the elderly. I push visions of people overdosed on prunes out of my mind. It is halfway through the movie. There is no line; no one will suffer for the sake of my sexual appetites. I may take double or triple my fair turn in the lavatory, and I will feel a little guilty about it. But for all they know, I could have a good reason to be in there. I could be constipated.

I slide the accordion door open. The automatic light turns on when the door is locked. I get the tripod out of my purse and set my phone up to record.

Coat off. I'm aiming at a swift undressing but in a manner that gives the camera a sense of languid sensuality. Buttons slide through holes. I pop my breasts out of their bra. I rub *mile-high madness*

the nipples gratuitously. Solo breast play does little for me. It's about as exciting as kissing my own hand. Showing off for an imagined audience does do something for me though, so maybe it's not entirely gratuitous, but I don't linger.

Hips shimmy to help work my panties and leggings down a few inches. That's all I need. My fingers are between my labia *tout suite*. Airplanes are loud. The engine rumbles, the ventilation hisses and the intercom dings for regular announcements.

I close my eyes and try to be fully present with my pussy.

My mind wanders. My eyes open. I move the camera about to get a better angle. The bathroom is tight and I can't get all of me in frame. I bend over so lips and tits join the frame for a moment, then I open my legs to the camera. I try a shot from below, as if the camera is looking up my skirt. This is a terrible up-nose angle for faces but for my pussy it's wonderful. I'm surprised at how beautiful my thighs are. A voice in my head is pretty certain it's just the camera angle. The near perfection I see must be illusion.

"Shhh, me."

Feel. Enjoy. Orgasm.

You are on a time limit here.

I back into the corner against the door hinges, the camera balanced on the toilet lid. I contort myself until seven-eighths of my pussy, half my face and all of my tits are showing. I feel the delicate skin. I think of everyone who might someday watch this video. I think of how embarrassing it would be. I think of what my pussy must look like.

I come.

I dress.

I flush the happy blue liquid down the toilet. I want it to

sound like I used the facilities for their intended purpose. I straighten my clothes. No one glares at me as I exit the lavatory, or if they do, I don't notice. I ease languidly down the aisle, back to my seat. As I buckle up, I realize I feel normal sized again.

I'll be having a relaxing finish to my flight.

Mile-High Madness is an essay inspired by filming and editing *Mile High Masturbation*, May 2016.

14

mommy's new toy

GUILT RUINS MOST OF MY SHOPPING TRIPS, especially if the person I'm shopping for is me. There's always something more important I'm supposed to be doing with money, like buying new tires or a winter coat for my daughter. But it just happens to be the second Saturday of May, and I grab at the excuse of Mother's Day to make a rare guilt-free purchase.

I'm still loyal to that same boutique sex shop that popped my porn cherry. I make a point of going into Oh My once or twice a year. I used to get so discombobulated just walking in the door that I could hardly speak, let alone think. Today I'm astonished at my clarity of mind. My voice is clear now and from the look on the woman's face, I'm coherent too. Bonus. It's the same woman I met at the college fair almost a decade ago. She listens intently as I tell her that the vibrator I have is just too vibraty.

"I have just the thing for you," she assures me.

It's small, about seven inches long, an inch wide and a half inch thick. You could use it as a bookmark, almost. It's soft, pink, flexible and silicone. It's Mommy's first clitoral vibrator.

At the checkout counter she remembers to give me a teacher's discount. I'm super impressed. I'd forgotten about the discount. Given the shit I put up with as a junior high math teacher, a discount on a little self-care is a lovely gesture, one that floods me with guilt. I accept the discount and try not to think of what some people might say.

I won't be able to use my new vibrator when I get home. First it has to get a good charge on it. I open the sexy packaging with reverence. Every little design detail turns me on. They've copied the best parts of Apple's iPhone box. Even the snug fit of the lid produces a tactile pleasure, the perfect amount of friction to make it come apart slow and seductive. The vibrator and its cord are magnetically attracted to each other, literally. There's a small white disk with two tiny metal protrusions and a round smooth receiving pad. I plug it in, eagerly anticipating Mother's Day. With the charging cord and receptor pad seated together in magnetic bliss, two little red lights alternate on and off. All night long their glow is a sexy little indication of the electrical charge building within.

In the morning I poach flowers from the yard. It was a family tradition growing up, an inexpensive gesture of love for my mom, one that three derelict children could always afford. I'm alone in these early hours of the morning, and I pick flowers for myself. With fur-lined boots and a coat over my silk nightgown, I head outside to relieve my lilac bushes of their burdensome blooms. Dew is heavy on the grass and the hedges. It's a gray morning. With old scissors, I gather a huge bouquet. Water droplets wet my hands and drip onto my chest. The lilacs smell like everything right in the world. They smell of wonder.

The vibrator lets go of its charger reluctantly. I savor the little tug required to separate them. I'm such a selfish girl interjecting myself between their magnetic bliss. I chuckle at the ridiculous stories in my head, and feel my pussy start to pulse in anticipation. But I won't start with my pussy. I'm savoring the morning.

I pose with the flowers in front of my crotch, legs wide in blatant here-I-am pussy pose, but my pussy is hiding behind the vase. I'm such a tease. But that's what Instagram requires, modesty of some variety. And I love it.

After a few happy still shots, I repose on the couch in my steel-blue silk nightie, determined to start Mother's Day off being spoiled. The cool silk slither is sexy on my skin. I run my hands over my breasts and turn on the vibrator with just one little squeeze.

I rub the vibrating end on my nipple to start, then put it in my mouth. What turns me on always goes in my mouth at one point or another—fingers, cocks and toys. But few of the toys that go in my mouth look so much like they belong there. This vibrator is curiously shaped like a doctor's tongue depressor. I put it in my mouth, thinking of the medical scenes I've imagined with naughty doctors who think an orgasm will cure my ennui. Unlike a wooden tongue depressor, this vibrator is bendy. A soft buzz fills my mouth along with the soft texture of silicone. It's a soft pink color too, stereotypically feminine in every way, and I love it. But I have no idea what to do with it. There's no real instruction manual. If there was, I probably wouldn't do more than glance at it anyway.

I have a master's degree in education and I'm a firm believer in experiential play.

I ponder this girly contraption. The buzzier part should go

on my clit, right?

I try it with my pussy toward the camera.

That shameless position is exciting, but the toy is not quite doing it for me. I wrap my legs into a proper position for a sitting lady. I stay that way and soak in the buzzy hum. Time is an element of stimulation. How intense will it get if I just wait and observe? I close my eyes. It's buzzy down there. I wait and I observe that this is silly. It feels good but not drive-me-to-orgasm good. I suppose that's not a bad thing. Good is good. There's nothing wrong with sitting around enjoying a pleasant feeling and seeing where it goes.

But I'm micro bored.

I open my legs again and squirm the nubby part around on my folds.

There are settings, with programmed vibrational sequences. I click from steady buzz to…how do you describe it? Morse code might work. I could say "four shorts and a long" or "a swooping acceleration followed by an infuriating pause." Bah. I let my hand show the sensation. My fingers flick with each surge of pussytastic pulsing.

I change the setting again. This one is like a mix between a dial tone and a revving engine. It's amusing but I click once more and am back at the first setting without having found a favorite.

I don't know about this toy. I want it to send me to the moon, but I'll be lucky if it even sends me as far as the barn. I don't like feeling stuck or stymied. I think for a moment.

"What would make this hotter?" I ask myself. "Lube?"

Mmm, better, but not good enough. You have to take your clothes off or something.

I slink out of the silk nightshirt. Nudity. That's embarrassing.

I writhe and wriggle for the camera, exaggerated movements drawing me into the moment.

Since flower petals worked on Valentine's Day, I grab a fistful of lilacs. Mmm, different, but still not doing it for me. I want this vibrator buried inside me. I insert the thicker end into my nether regions and fold the nubby part over my clit. I stretch my pussy lips over it as much as possible. Just a slip of pink shows out of my slit and through my fingers.

There's still no orgasm on the horizon as far as I can see.

I give up on trying to make the toy give me one. I close my eyes and work on giving myself one.

Hot scenarios. Come on, baby, think up some hot scenarios... I think of being forced to eat pussy. I reverse the scenario and imagine receiving oral from a woman forced to eat me. I stack me and this unwilling woman up on a bed ready for fucking in turns by a nameless wonder of a lover. Yeah, that's a good one. She and I are both suddenly eager and willing.

He's in my pussy, he's in her pussy, he's in my pussy. No! Stay in mine, I say with my eager hips. He goes back to hers. Not fair.

My fingers start their circles and I masturbate with the clit vibrator in exactly the same way I would without it. Circles, circles and more circles.

"Let's see who comes first," he says to us. I'm dying to orgasm. He shoves his cock back inside me. It's wet with her juice. He is double, triple and quadruple dipping. I hold her tight on top of me. I can feel her breasts jiggle with the reverberations of the pounding he's giving me. I bite her shoulder medium hard. She gasps and smiles. I want this forever.

He pulls out and I feel his rhythm through her body. I grab her breast, a big handful. She is glorious. I walk my fingers to her nipple and squeeze, slowly looking for that sweet spot where her body tells me it's just maybe too much. She turns her head and kisses me. I'm the luckiest woman alive. The outsides of her thighs rub the insides of mine and she starts to groan. She's going to come. She's going to come. She's going to come. Oh, God. I'm coming with her. He pulls out of her and rams into me.

An orgasm ripples through me. My hips push into the rhythm. Waves of pleasure and contractions continue. This was a good one.

After a few dazed moments on the couch, I look at the pink thing in my hand. Huh. Well. I like my new toy, I think. Wait. Actually, I'm not sure it's so much the toy as the playing. I like to play, and I like anything that gives me an excuse to play with myself, including this toy. What a wonderful Mother's Day treat.

Mommy's New Toy is an essay inspired by filming and editing *Mother's Day*, May 2016.

15

invisibilized

IT'S A DICK. A hairy dick. And it's shiny in the "I just took a picture of my oiled dick with the flash on" kind of way. I sigh, not surprised at the unappealing image. I get ten dicks a day, despite the "No DM" policy statement at the top of my Instagram account. And most of them have zero artistic merit.

I ignore the photo but feel validated. The world needs better dick pics and I've just started a side project to address the issue. I've been taking my own dick pics. Unlike this unfortunate, I don't send them to people without asking, but I do take them. I love my dick pics more than I'd ever have imagined.

My collection of strap-ons has doubled, and I've got at least five attachments now, two of which are flaccid. One hundred percent of the unsolicited dick pics I've gotten have been of hard cocks, as if erections are the only thing to be proud of. I love cock in all its glorious variations. I want my dick pics to reflect that.

The first lover I had, after fifteen years of monogamy, was significantly older than myself. He usually maintained an erection, but not always. On those times when he couldn't I had so much fun slurping his flaccid cock and luxuriating in the joy of human touch without the drive to orgasm. I hoped to relieve the fear of inadequacy I saw in his eyes.

Now that I have a flaccid dildo, I've been thinking about sucking my old lover's limp cock. Being the social justice do-gooder that I am, I want to make a social service announcement via YouTube in support of sexuality even in the face of impotence, be it periodic or otherwise. Not a preachy one that says, "Even if you can't get a hard-on, there's lots of great ways to get and give pleasure." I want to announce loudly that I love limp cock. That in whatever state, a cock is worthy of love. I want to present a counter narrative to the pressure of performance.

I set my packers out on the bed and delight in their wiggliness. I'd never have guessed how fun I'd find it to own fake penises. I didn't know what to buy, or what I'd like, so I came home with a variety. Not long ago this would have been impossible. A smile down at the pink little flaccid cocks, and I feel gratitude to the pioneering queer and trans folk whose efforts lend me this unexpected perk. I won't ever wear one to put a bulge in my pants, but running around naked with a flaccid cock strapped on sounds like a romping good time.

I bought a small and a medium. The flesh tones are close, but not exact matches. One is too pink, the other too yellow. Their springiness makes them far more realistic than the hard strap-ons I have. Real cocks always have sproinginess, even when hard as a rock. I like these because they are soft. I always feel a bit pressured around a hard cock.

Lack of pressure is figurative and literal as it pertains to penises, or penes. I wonder if you can measure an erection's pressure? If so would you use psi, like for a tire? Or is it more like blood pressure, and you'd use mmHg? I thought blood pressure was a whole-body thing, but maybe an erection is localized hypertension. Either way, in pounds per square inch or in millimeters of mercury, I'd like some data, 'cause I'm just that kind of girl.

I get my tripod and camera set. I don't feel like I have time to make a video, but I never have time. It's now or never; the stream of ideas runs too strong to wait until later. This one will be swept downstream in the torrent if I don't shoot it now. I'm in frame while seated on my bed. It's obvious I have no makeup on. I look like shit. Oh well. My friend who's an internet coach says her "worst" videos are always the most popular. "Viewers don't want to see you polished," she says. "They want raw truth."

I take a deep breath and press record.

"I love limp cock," I tell the camera. I jiggle and wiggle the squishy disembodied penis in my hand and pop it in my mouth. The initial taste of talc gives way to slurpy ease. Limp cock doesn't trigger my gag reflex; it has so much texture to explore and it's so comforting. It's like comfort food minus the calories. I thought I loved limp cock because all the nerve endings were still there minus performance anxiety, but a packer penis has no attached cerebral cortex and I'm getting excited anyway. Sucking it makes me wet.

You are disgusting.
What the fuck?
Amazing.
Bat-shit, why the fuck am I getting hard?
I wouldn't let that bitch near my cock.
She can suck mine.
I've got eight inches of steel for you babe.

I read the comments with equanimity. YouTube trolls are easy enough to ignore, but I'm surprised that none of them seem to get it. I'm disappointed. The reason I posted this video seems lost on them. I guess I need to be more pedantic. Maybe that's the reason preachers are so preachy.

Maybe my script should have read something more like, "I love cock, hard or limp, but my experience with older men is that an erectionless penis makes them feel inadequate. That's not a sexy feeling, and it doesn't lead to pleasure, joy or a stiffy. Sitting back and enjoying a good slobbery mess of a blowjob often does. And if it doesn't, it still feels damn good to be touched, from what I hear. I posted the video as a statement of affirmation for all kinds of sexual experience."

Here I am, waving my flag of sex positivity and guys are just evaluating my fuckability. They must be young and stupid. Maybe one day, when they can't get it up, they'll think back on that crazy YouTube and feel a little less inadequate because someone once said she loves limp cock.

I really do. I love cock in all its variations. The speed at which a cock can change, and the number of states there are between flaccid and full tilt, are wonders of the world.

I can sympathize with being stuck on the flaccid side of the spectrum. I can relate to a feeling of impotence. I feel impotent as the divorce drags on and on. I can't comprehend how two people who theoretically agreed on a fifty-fifty split can't in actuality settle anything, not even with a mediator. The anticipated couple of months has already turned into nine months with no end in sight. Waiting for the legal aspect of divorce to resolve feels like my ex has control of my life. It's miserable. But I really, really don't want a relationship until I'm free and clear.

Hookups seem like a good compromise.

"Ha, ha, I'm sex positive too" is a common response I get on my dating profile. I'm just looking for hookups, nothing more. Apparently, the phrase "sex positive" is not widely understood. I live in such a liberal bubble. Despite the fact that I'm looking for casual sex, most guys want dinner first. Weird.

"I've been single almost a year," I tell him. Saying I've been single is a simplification. "Singleish" is more accurate—mostly single, idealistically single, in some ways logistically single, but by no means perfectly single. I was aiming at celibacy until the divorce is done, but I can't take it any longer. It's become unhealthy, yet another way I can't move on until he cooperates.

I want to get laid.

I'm sitting in a fine New England restaurant. This man with adorably striped socks who arrives at a first date with a rose is an attentive listener.

"I only had sex with four people before I got married. I was monogamous for fifteen years. And I've only been with two men since."

As I hear myself describing how few people I've slept with, I'm appalled. This is a claim for purity. I look at the red wine swirling in my glass. I'm scared to be seen as promiscuous. It's the same kind of shame that made masturbating difficult. Fuck me.

The red wine smells wonderful.

"So, you're an engineer?" I prod. It's best if I just stop talking now.

"Yes."

"What kind of projects do you work on?" I ask.

"I work on packaging, waste reduction and whatever anyone hires the company to invent."

I prod further. He says that some plastics really don't give off harmful chemicals when heated. I believe he believes it, but I don't. I was raised to distrust plastic. It's dead dinosaurs, for Christ's sake. It's like desecrating an ancient cemetery. Petroleum products are creepy.

I don't mention my misgivings. He's interesting, smart and a decent listener. Conversation flows, the lights are dim and his red hair looks more attractive in person than I expected. I like him. We take an after-dinner stroll, admire the trees and the moon. We hold hands.

In my need to be honest and forthright I tell him about my online project. I don't want him to think I'm normal and get an unpleasant surprise after we've fucked. I don't want him to feel betrayed. He might be freaked that anyone on the planet with Internet access can see me naked and masturbating. I'd rather be disappointed than risk disapproval later. It's a preemptive strike on being shamed.

"I was raised with a lot of sexual shame and repression," I tell him. "After I became single again, I realized I was still ashamed to even masturbate. I decided to investigate that with a yearlong commitment to masturbating once a week on film."

"That's awesome!" he says, and squeezes my hand. His hands are warm and dry.

He tells me how he wishes that his ex-wife were more like me. And he shares that he masturbates every day.

"Every day?" I ask, blushing in the dark. Every day. Suddenly my goal of once a week seems smaller than small peanuts.

Talk of masturbation hijacks the conversation, permanently. It's hard to get him to talk of anything else, except maybe sex. We almost fuck in the backseat of his car, because he doesn't want to spring for a hotel. I'm not going to have a man I just met over to my house. He could be stalker material for all I know, and I have a daughter, even if she's not home right now.

We text another week or two and then I drive to the city to visit him for a weekend. I feel a little weird as he announces that he's set up a camera to film us while we have sex. He should ask me if it's okay with me. But I don't want to ruin the moment.

"I can't believe you're looking at the camera while I'm entering you for the first time," he complains.

What did he expect? My films are fabulous because I take care in creating them. He's been watching them all week. Didn't he notice?

The moment is kind of ruined even without me speaking up. He's obviously totally ignorant about how much work goes into making my videos.

The sex is good, though, and there is plenty of it. The food is good too.

How was your day? I ask.

Good, he texts back. *Are you masturbating right now?*

His question surprises and hurts. I'd like to talk about my day. One class got totally absorbed in measuring, plotting the growing daffodils out front. It's a great way to get reluctant kids fluent with fractions while still wrestling with higher-order thinking and grade-level content, like proportionality, and the difference between an independent and dependent variable. The other class, not so much. I got shoved around by a student. Admin is in denial about the level of violence. I was physically shaking at work today. Was it in fear, exhaustion, frustration or overwhelm? I don't know. And this guy asks if my fingers are in my twat.

First things first, I guess. Fuck him for making men the stereotype of men.

Fuck him. I am a whole person. He knows that. He's not some fan. I've shown him other parts of me. I started with other parts of me.

I'd like to be asked how my day was, or how I am, or if anything interesting happened in my day. Open-ended questions are good. I know this guy is capable of interesting conversation.

At least he was before sex was introduced into the equation.

I stand up for myself. I do the math for him. "I masturbate on film about an hour each week, out of approximately ninety-eight waking hours. One divided by ninety-eight is 0.98, or ninety hundredths. That's ninety-eight per hundred or ninety-eight percent. It's not likely that you'll catch me masturbating. It's how I spend less than two percent of my time."

"Okay," he says.

A week later, I invite him to my place. I'm washing dishes. His arms come around me from behind. I love when a man kisses the back of my neck while I'm in the kitchen. I smile so big and happy. His hands glide around my waist and my shirt flips up over my tits. My boobs are hanging out for the neighbors to see. It's dark outside and the light over the sink is on. I might as well be on a large-screen television. Or in a fishbowl with a spotlight.

"Don't," I say.

"What?" he says. "You're an exhibitionist." He doesn't ask, he states. His tone is dismissive or mocking. I'm flustered.

"These are my neighbors, and they didn't consent," I explain to him. People who watch my videos *choose* to watch my videos. The distinction is important. It seems lost on him.

I decline an offer to meet up again. I'd rather do chores than get groped again by Mr. Redhead with bad boundaries. I need to film anyway. "Ha, ha, fuck it. I'm going to film myself doing chores." There's dirty clothes all over my bedroom floor. I put an extra sway in my hips as I pick them up. I adjust the tie on my robe suggestively and head to the basement.

I get one camera low to the ground for an upshot on my pussy and another a few feet back for a full-body shot. I make sure its line of sight just misses the other camera. I'm rubbing out a good one on the washing machine when the spin cycle hits. It works, it really works.

Not all urban legends are myth.

I'm sad and lonely, but at least the laundry is done. And the footage is fucking fantastic.

I lose my phone, and his contact info with it. I'm relieved.

Invisibilized is an essay inspired by filming and editing *Laundry Day: Orgasm on the Spin Cycle*, June 2016.

16

i love you, daddy

IT IS SUNDAY, filming day and Father's Day. The clear light of dawn promises beautiful sunny skies. The heat of the day looms and threatens but its real smackdown is hours away. I will not be wishing anyone a happy Father's Day this year—not my dad, not my ex-husband, and not the kinky daddy I am no longer talking to. If you'd told me a couple years ago that I had "daddy issues," I'd have given you a blank stare. Now I'm scratching my head in consternation. Clearly, I have daddy issues but I'm not sure what they are or what to do about them. And I'm not going to figure it out in one day. I could, however, do a little emotional investigation. I need to make my masturbation film anyway, so why not take all the parts of my day and mash 'em together?

I'm full of a weird mix of sadness and hope as I resign myself to paying attention to what comes up as I film today. I wish I didn't have daddy issues but I do. I wish I knew why, so I could get over it.

I pack my film equipment and quiver a little. I can't help but imagine the mountain of judgments "normal" people will lob at me. I leave the house wearing a frilly pink-and-white-checked

i love you, daddy

dress with a matching petticoat. My long blonde braids dangle past my shoulders and bounce up and down as I go. Their ends are tied with big white satin ribbons. The larger tripod swings along in one hand and a second smaller one hides in the backpack. I worry I'll have sweat staining the small of my back and my armpits by the time I reach the park at the top of the hill.

The houses on either side of the street are quiet. I imagine what early risers in the neighborhood are thinking, looking out their windows at a woman with her hair in two braids walking down the street in a square-dancing dress at dawn. It's not likely they'd assume I'm filming naughty kinky things, but my heart races and my hands sweat. Do I look like a sex pervert, or someone who got their holidays confused and thinks it's Halloween in June?

I bought this dress in my teens at Goodwill. It's always looked like a toddler dress to me, like the ones Nana bought me at Easter. Pink, frilly babygirl. I wore it as a doll costume for Halloween in college. I'd never have guessed I'd be wearing it twenty years later to film myself masturbating in the neighborhood park. Nor that I'd be doing research for a book on masturbation as a means to shedding my own sexual shame. And not in a million billion years would I have guessed I'd end up accidentally producing indie feminist porn.

But more than all those combined, I never imagined myself as a kinky babygirl. There's no probability whatsoever that in college I could have guessed age play would emerge as one of my kinks. I hadn't even heard of it. I remained ignorant until just a couple years ago.

The first rivulets of sweat run down my back as I crest the top of the hill. The park is empty but for a lone guy walking his dog toward the woods. Mist hangs around the edges of the park like a frame. Just beyond the fog, cars whiz by on the freeway. I get to work in a giddy rush. I place one tripod at the foot of the slide for an up-the-skirt shot, and the other I position for a side view. I start the cameras rolling and playtime begins.

The skin on the backs of my thighs sticks to the slide a bit. I shove the petticoats under my ass, lean back and go down with a smile on my face. I am a bad girl and my bare feet grip well enough to get me all the way back up the slide the wrong way. I pant at the top awhile and feel the cargo nets calling me. "Come play," they say.

I move my cameras from the slide to the bridge made of cargo nets.

My bare feet stretch and work to grip the web of nylon straps. I try to make it look sexy. It's difficult to get panties or cleavage showing, disappointingly so. For such a short skirt, this dress gives an awful lot of coverage. I move the camera again and again as I try all the playground equipment. For innocently naughty poses, the wall of metal climbing loops is the best. I bend over the curved bars and delight in parting my legs wide to climb through. This produces an excellent crotch shot. My innocent white panties are getting plenty of footage. I go all the way to the top of the climbing rings, knees bending, bare legs and toes dangling free. I am princess of the world, crowned in morning's glow, my pussy full of intent and possibility.

But it's hard for the camera to see up so high, so it's a private moment of glory. And then I climb down, adjust the cameras and play some more.

Swings! Legs pumping, braids flying, I lean way back and pump hard. Big swings. Oh, that makes me feel sick. I lean so

i love you, daddy

far, the small of my back is on the seat. My legs wrap around the chains in the air, white-pantied butt framed in petticoat ruffles. I twist the chains and they unwind, my braids flying out to the sides. I thunk to a stop, sit up and drag my toes in the dirt. Forward and back, forward and back, like a wobbly pendulum.

I could make a whole movie just on this swing. Part of me could stay here forever. In a parallel universe I'm probably still there, happiness in perpetuity.

The quintessential thing about a very young age is that you haven't learned shame yet. You haven't learned about sex. You lift your skirts because a breeze on your belly is fun. But at thirty-nine, I am both innocent and naughty.

Time presses. I need to be done before any real kids arrive. Sequestered in the little play hut, I do the splits, putting my legs as provocatively wide as they go, which is pretty damn wide. I smile coy flirtations at the camera and wrap my braids around my head. I stick the ends in my mouth. I look around, making sure no one will find me out, then I pull my panties aside. I want to play with myself but I do not feel safe in the park. I'm not hidden enough.

I go home.

I find a better hiding place.

Hiding is a key part of doing bad things as a child. I remember hiding behind a tree in the cow pasture when I was in first grade. I was looking at myself the best I could, pants around my calves. For whatever reason, curiosity I suppose, I placed a stone between my labia and held it there. I didn't know words like "labia," "yoni" or "pussy." I might have thought "vagina." But with dread certainty, I knew that if my father found out what I was up to, I'd be in trouble.

Touching myself was a punishable offense.

Today, I set my cameras under the pear tree in the backyard. One I toss in the grass to squat over as I rub myself, and the other I place with care on a tripod. The sky is a perfect blue and the grass knee high with neglect. It's the perfect little-girl hideaway, between the branches reaching down and the long grass growing up. I pull off my panties and toss them aside. I start working my fingers over my happy-go-lucky.

I rub and rub and rub. That's what I do because I don't orgasm easily. And then I know, I know just what will make me come. I pick a little bouquet of grass and place it between my labia, just as I had with that stone when I was a child.

I imagine the people who will see this naughty transgression.

The bouquet is delicate and lacy. It stays put remarkably well. My sticky pussy holds it with surety. The bouquet quivers with me as I rub. I know I look weird but I feel beautiful. Actually, I know I look beautiful too, to anyone who's let their judginess go, even just a little. I'm embarrassed and grateful and there isn't a thought in my mind as my boobs jiggle and my fingers work like crazy. It's a beautiful day in the neighborhood. My mouth opens in the gaping-fish pose that means I'm about to come. My arm and leg muscles go stiff, my eyes pop open and my groin explodes with a magic ball of pleasure.

Yup, sure enough, the bouquet tips me over into eye-rolling orgasm. How is it that the little voice inside of me always finds just what I need?

Naughty girl, I like you.

I Love You, Daddy is an essay inspired by filming and editing *Father's Day in the Park*, June 2016.

17

self-edited

"CLEAR YOUR PLATE," I tell my daughter.

"I was going to," she answers back.

Teenagers, I think. But I drop it there. She doesn't like reminders. Note taken.

I'm the one who needs reminders anyway. It's seven p.m. and I haven't even started editing. I want to go buy some ice cream for an after-dinner treat. Instead I shuffle off to my bedroom.

My daughter knows not to enter my room if the laptop is open. She was eager to get on my new MacBook when I bought it last December. Age-appropriate honesty is how I've raised my daughter. She's a teenager now and doesn't need coddling.

"There are naked pictures of me on this computer, and videos," I told her.

It was an odd moment of embarrassment and courage, as a parent. My daughter looked surprised, then laughed.

"Do you have any questions about the work I'm doing?" I asked.

"No," she said.

From then on she acted like my laptop was mildly radioactive. She never even asked to use my computer again. In my experience, no kid wants to see their parent having sex, in person or on film. As an added precaution, I keep a password on my computer and my bedroom door closed while editing.

I don't want to be in my bedroom with the door closed right now. I want to curl up on the couch and watch a movie. I think my videos should magically edit themselves.

Blarg. Seriously, I don't want to edit.

I'll be fine, though, once I get started. I put my headphones on and start transferring files from my camera. I got great footage of the children's train at the park when we took my niece there yesterday. I'm going to use that non-sexual imagery for an artsy intro. It'll be fabulous but…I don't want to do the work. I want it to be done already.

"Shut up," I tell myself. My thoughts are annoyingly repetitive.

It's easier to do anything besides sitting down to edit. But that's why God created deadlines. I glance at the clock in the corner of my screen. It says seven-thirteen p.m. Monday is five hours away and I have an hour of footage from each camera. That's easily three hours of editing. And then there's music, credits and polishing.

I answer an email and send a few texts.

"I have to edit," I tell myself.

But first, I have to go pee.

And I need a cup of tea.

When I get back to my computer, I'm dumbfounded to find midnight only four hours away. I have to get started, for real. I import the footage to iMovie and look for the distinctive pattern in the sound lines where I orgasm. The timing is always off by the amount of time it took for me to get from one camera to the next as I turned them on. The orgasm vocalizations are the easiest common event to identify in both reels of footage. The editing software shows the footage in two stacked strips, one on top of the other, like piano music. I line the frames up perfectly, to the hundredth of a second. I get the footage synced and my brain spurts dopamine, giving me a little happy-juice high. I'm settling in and getting into a good workflow.

"Mom, snuggle me."

Shit. I'm on mom duty.

Good moms tuck their daughters into bed, and my daughter deserves a good mom.

"Five minutes of snuggles," I say.

I have the coolest kid in the world—fifteen and she still wants an occasional cuddle. I'm excited to see what an awesome life she's going to live. I turn off her light, wrap my arms around her and think to myself, *I love this girl.* After a few minutes I sneak away quietly.

"Stay," she says. I'm totally incapable of being sneaky.

"Can't," I say. "I have to edit."

By the time I get back to work, it's ten o'clock already. Shit. Two hours to my editing deadline. And I should be going to bed. How does this happen?

I'm glad I have the park footage to jazz up the actual masturbation scene. I had a stomachache when I was filming. I didn't feel well at all. But a girl has to film when she has the time. During my window of opportunity, I lie in bed wearing plain cotton panties. They are embarrassingly old and ratty tatty. But I watch the film and see that I worked those undies for all they were worth. And it worked. I teased with them, poked my fingers under, almost pulled them aside, gave myself a wedgie and, of course, rubbed them all over my clit.

No one is ever going to find these panties sexy, I think to myself. But I know I'm wrong. Everything is somebody's kink.

Besides, trying to be sexy to others isn't my goal. I constantly remind myself that my goal is to be real, however I am, and to masturbate, no fake, no phony, no full of baloney. My inner Yoda lectures me that "There is no try. Only do."

I am sexy. It's an immutable fact. I just have to access it, and let it be seen.

Doubt is sexiness's worst enemy. I kept doubt at bay long enough to orgasm while filming, now I just have to stay clear long enough to edit and post the video. I look at the screen. It's just me in my bed, again. Fuck. How am I going to make this video engaging?

Philosophically, my goal is to live unedited, but in a practical world, no one has time for that shit. I have to edit. I have to shape and pace the story without sacrificing the integrity of telling it real and raw.

In the beginning, I was afraid cutting any part of a scene would make me guilty of creating yet another idealized version of sexuality. I didn't want to skip the not-so-pretty parts of sex. And I wanted a true portrayal of how long it takes for me to orgasm, but not at the price of boring my audience. For the first few months, I didn't cut anything. I'd just use the fast-forward mode to tighten thirty minutes down to fifteen.

I trust myself more now. I cut this footage liberally, while making sure to leave in a few embarrassing tidbits, like the upward-facing dog I did as a pre-masturbation warm-up. I also leave in the jiggling-belly-fat scene.

I am going to be up so freaking late. There's too much footage.

For the first few months, I was a seventeen-minute girl. Lately, I've been averaging more like forty-five minutes to climax. Ironic.

In theory, taking longer to orgasm just means more foreplay and more sensual pleasure. It doesn't sound like something to complain about, but orgasming faster means less footage to edit. And I want to go to bed.

I scroll through the footage, watching myself move as if on fast-forward. I've completely failed to gain more control over my orgasms. I'd expected a committed masturbation practice would result in my ability to come faster and more consistently. Instead it's getting harder for me to come.

How fucked up is that?

In what kind of practice do you get worse at the thing you're practicing? It's probably a sign of depression, but I'm not as depressed as I would be without the practice. Realistically, if it weren't for this project, I'd go months and months at a time without masturbating and not even realize it. Setting aside even this small amount of joy for myself is probably the smartest thing I'm doing this year.

I watch myself rubbing my belly and then my breasts, comfort spots.

Dismissing my own feelings is a bad habit. I'm trying to forge a new one. I take a breath and rethink things. My whole life, down to my masturbation practice, feels like swimming in molasses. That is an indicator of depression. I won't hide that, nor will I cry myself a river. When a slower orgasm is one of your leading flags for depression, you're a pretty lucky duck.

I make a longer, slower intro than usual, even though the whole thing feels fast with the time-lapse effect. Usually I drop a title frame in after about six seconds. I start this one with six seconds of a train rumbling by, then give a time-lapse effect, so you get the idea I've been in bed and restless awhile. Only after twenty seconds do I present two words—"sad heart"—and the intro continues. Light shifts over my prone form in the bed as clouds pass outside the window. This is definitely an artsy masturbation video.

At a minute and a half I add the words "achy tummy" on an otherwise black screen. I pet my poor tummy. I add a few words here and there, on a black screen, like an old silent film. The next frames say, "Tummy hurts. No feels good." I hope the audience hears a voice similar to the one in my head, a cute sick kid using improper sentence structure because that's what young kids do. I hope it's endearing rather than idiotic. Nothing I can do about it. I can't pretend to have someone else's ideas.

With the fast speed and silent-era feel, the video is humorous. I like that, but it's also a bit flattening. It's not like I want to make people sad. I definitely *don't* want to make people sad. Sadness equals limp dicks and forlorn clits. But I don't want to ignore the true emotional content. If I did focus on the sad, I'd mess that up probably. It would come off as glorifying depression.

I'm not looking at the camera at all in this footage. I'm ignoring it. That's unusual. Depression might not be the only contributing factor to my slower climax. For the first few months, being in front of the camera was an event unto itself, and so taboo. But as I grow more comfortable in front of the camera, it commands less of my attention. It alone used to keep me laser focused. Ironically, I thought I was slow then, and that was embarrassing too. I'm slower now but I find that fact more frustrating than embarrassing. The latter is much sexier than the former.

It's not just the taboo; I was happier at the beginning of this project. The first few months of freedom after I moved out were intoxicating, before the legal process of the divorce derailed.

With the editing software, I create a slow pan in on my pussy at the point where I pull my panties aside. With my knees over my chest, my pussy looks more like a hole than a slit. It's inviting. I'm getting wet editing this. And still I'm sad.

The increasing hostilities between our lawyers has been hell. The lawyer's bills mean I can't leave my day job, and that's killing me. I've spent almost twenty thousand dollars on lawyers. I assume my husband's costs are similar. That's probably half our life savings, burned. We are squandering our daughter's inheritance just a couple years before she goes to college.

It's not a sexy thought. Divorce is depressing, and that means more work to orgasm, and more editing time required. Less sleep turns into more sadness. I'm so stuck. But I have no idea how to be real about it, other than a few melancholy hints.

I can't really leave the audience sad, or myself sad, because that's not orgasmic. My commitment here is to masturbate once a week, and thank God, because if I didn't have this project...I can't imagine. I shudder and spill my tea. Fuck. Thank God, I missed my computer.

I need to get focused on editing. I'm only ten minutes into the footage. I scroll to the end and edit the orgasm. It helps my mental game. If the start is done, and the end is done, then I just have to scan the middle for the important parts. And if not all the best parts make it in, ah well, at least I'll be done and can freaking go to bed.

All I need to do is add music and credits, and I'm done. I'm too broke to figure out licensing and royalties, or whatever legal shit people have to do for a real soundtrack. Usually I use old classical music that's copyright free, but this video needs something else. "Hobo's Lullaby" has been running through my brain since that train ride yesterday. It's the perfect kind of sweet and melancholy for this video. But to use it legally, I'll have to sing it myself. I gather my mic and a songbook for lyrics. I can't sing up here. My bedroom is too close to my daughter's. I used to sing this song to her when she was an infant. Before that I used to sing it to her father. We were both hobo-smitten idealists. We even tried to hop a freight train together once.

Ironic that in the midst of the hardest year of my life, I try to find my truest self through art and writing only to end up with a collection of orgasm videos. I'm not sure what that says about me. But I definitely get a fail on communicating with full authenticity. Fans see a weekly moment of orgasmic glory and they think I'm a quirky sex bunny.

But hey, I get to share what I can with them. And in return they share their gratitude with me. I am a fuck ton happier than I'd be otherwise. I'm not being dishonest. It's more like the vector of sharing is imperfect, and the content too complex to convey. My videos can't say everything I want them to say. I am at a loss for how to deal with anger and sadness. So far I can only drop hints and jokes. That's all I've got for now.

Music, that's the answer to melancholy.

I sit on an old bucket in the basement. I hope I won't wake

my daughter from down here. I sing when I'm sad, always have. It's like going for a swim in the rain. The basement is the closest thing I have to a sound studio. I sing under the fluorescent lights with my eyes closed to the cobwebs, shelves of tools, old toys and spare insulation.

"Lift your head and smile at trouble. You'll find happiness someday."

I sing my hobo song with bare legs sticking out of boxer shorts. It's a one-take wonder. I don't have time for anything else.

I lay the soundtrack starting a ways in. The first several seconds I score with only the sounds of the train. I repeat the song at the credits. Ugh. The song is so short. I wish I could hire a composer, a guitar player and camera crew, and possibly people to edit. If I had money, people to edit would be amazing. I'd be asleep right now.

Sleeping. God that sounds really good.

I check the timestamp of the yet-untouched footage: forty-five minutes, thirty-three seconds. Fucky, fucky, fuck, fuck. Fuckleywuckitts. Ficklediwookettes. I'm tired. I'll go to bed as soon as I get a rough cut. When the camera started rolling I wasn't turned on. It's hard when you aren't turned on in the first place, it's harder still when you don't feel well, and triply so when you're sad.

I drag the cursor along the footage, scanning for interesting moments and facial expressions. I let my cursor play at normal speed for a moment. I watch myself pull my panties off, drop them on my face and inhale. That stays in for sure. I cut to the higher-angle camera as I pull my math t-shirt up over my bare breasts. They glow with perfection. I can't believe those are my goofy boobs. They don't look goofy, they look glorious. Must be the angle, and the lighting. Damn, the lighting is so fucking sexy.

I crop out the bits where I got up to adjust the cameras and plunk in a few fade-to-black transitions. There are several transition options but generally I don't like the crossfade, blur, or fade to white. A transition, like a blink, should remain unnoticed. The less it draws attention, the more likely it's doing its job well.

I blink. My eyes are scratchy. I should be sleeping. I skip back to the orgasm. I almost always laugh or giggle right after an orgasm. I have no idea why. It wasn't something I was conscious of before I started filming myself. And I had no idea I did this before I started watching the footage of myself. It warms my heart to know that I can't orgasm without smiling, and to hear myself giggle with the joy of orgasm, even when I'd started out so sad.

If I keep rubbing my eyes, I'm going to have to finish this in the morning. I can't see and rub my eyes at the same time. On screen, I suck my toes like a baby for a moment. I love the angle my leg makes, especially with the camera pointing at my pussy and ass. It's so disarming, and seemingly unselfconscious. I just filmed this and I can't remember if I was self-conscious at that moment. I think not. I'd remember if I was. I'm worried about the sad parts. And the getting this done.

I switch to split screen so I can see both images at the same time in the view window. Usually I choose one or the other for the final product, switching to pussy shots whenever I make a dumb face or look obviously at the other camera. It's like you can tell I'm making eye contact with someone else—bad, bad, bad girl. I've got great pussy close-ups and face shots. I run them side by side. Let the viewers' eyes go where they will. And let me get my stupid ass to bed.

I rewatch the edit of the orgasm. I'm happy with my choice

self-edited

of the face shot. I never know which to show during orgasm, the face or the pussy. Sometimes I do both in a split screen. This time I follow the face orgasm with an "instant replay" of the pussy footage. It's a choose your own adventure.

I put the pussy footage second, because my face has fewer blemishes. Tiny patches of cellulite on my ass become visible at the height of each contraction as my glutes squeeze. So tempting to edit that out, but I've done plenty of films with tight, pussy-only close-ups. I am documenting who I am, I tell myself, who I really am, warts included…or cellulite, as it were. I cringe and move the fuck on.

I drop the generic credits template in after my orgasm. I used to spend time thinking up cute credits like at the end of *Car Talk* on National Public Radio, but now I just type the first thing that comes to mind. I do every aspect of the film, editing and production, so it's all just silliness. I credit myself as the Train Rider, Clit Toucher and Crier, also as the Camera Girl and Errand Boy.

Fuckity muck muck, this is the hard part. Usually I put bloopers at the very end, after the credits, but nothing funny happened. If not bloopers, I usually have some other silly thing I did after the orgasm, like blowing kisses to the camera, but fuckity fuck fuck fucks. I didn't do anything sweet, or silly. I cried. Spontaneous sad tears. Last time I showed tears on my Instagram, I thought my fans' compassion nearly killed a few of them. I had to spend so much time reassuring them, I got scared off sharing the hard stuff.

In the beginning of this project, I cropped tears out of a video and I've felt I made the wrong choice ever since. Fuckity fuckwits, flummoxy flem flums.

I'll put it in. It's decided.

The orgasm is over. My breasts are covered. The word "Mathematicians" is recognizable on the front. I got that at a conference I presented at. It was a freebie from the Texas Instruments booth, a promo for their newest scientific calculator.

I'm stalling. I don't want to show tears.

I drop a warning in: "not suitable for some audiences." It's vague, but at least they can't say I didn't warn them. That's some comfort when you're upset, right? Probably not. But I'm mean, and that's my sense of humor. I'm too tired to edit out the tears. And I don't want to. I don't want to see them. It's three minutes. I just cut from ass to face and then let it run. Nasty teary wearies.

It's one a.m. already. It's Monday. I'm going to bed. I'm so done.

I sleep now.

Self-Edited is an essay inspired by filming and editing *Smile at Trouble*, July 2016.

18

camera whore

I SLIP PAST THE CAMERA into the shower. It's small but nicely tiled. The bathmat is going to get soaked; there's no helping it. I can't get a good clear shot of the piss running down my leg with the door shut.

I have to pee so bad.

But I can't yet. I have to set up the second camera. I'm riding the momentum of FetishCon to squelch my inner resistance.

I wrap the rubbery legs of the gorilla tripod around the top rail of the shower door. I hope really, really hard that the steam doesn't fuck the camera up. I look into the reflection of my eyes in the camera screen. I'm ambivalent, excited and nervous.

"Piss is like kink-light," I tell my squeamish parts. Compared to some of the fetishes on display at the conference, it's true. I'm not even sure piss is a kink. Oh, wait, that's the definition. A kink is getting off on something that's not considered normal to derive sexual pleasure from. It makes sense that I don't even know if piss is a kink. I've only ever thought of urine in utilitarian terms.

From Roman times to Colonial times, urine was one of the

most readily available and effective cleaning agents. It's a natural source of ammonia. In pre-industrial times, it was collected and widely used for all kinds of cleaning from teeth whitening to laundry. Basically, people have been playing with their piss since the dawn of time.

Shower pissing is actually something I've done for years as an environmentalist, but I never thought it erotic. I'm practical. I like saving toilet paper and a flush by goin' in the shower. I've only been self-conscious about it since I saw a *Seinfeld* episode where George gets ridiculed for pissing in the shower at the gym. Dread of public exposure for being a shower pisser rubbed off on me in just one episode.

Outing oneself is one way to oust a fear. Ironically, I'm outing myself for a kink I probably don't have. This video is an announcement that even if watersports becomes a kink of mine, I respect myself unconditionally. I won't hide.

Oh my God, I hope I pee well enough to live up to these lofty expectations.

The tiles are cool on the bottoms of my feet. My warm piss will join the milieu soon. I do my best and most impressive peeing in the morning. That's when it's the yellowest. Sometimes the stream is so thick and forceful I can't help thinking, *I piss like a racehorse.* That's probably why I never get urinary tract infections.

I want to get my stance right. I swivel my hips. Should I be straight on to the camera, or at an angle? I don't know what's sexier, one big stream, legs spread, or legs together and piss running down them. I'll only have one chance at getting this first pee of the day. I'm afraid I'm going to mess up. There will be no second take. I can't wait hours to fill my bladder again.

I wonder if people do fake pee for professional fetish films. This convention would be the place to ask. What would fake pee be made of, a mix of apple juice and vinegar? Would you warm it, so it doesn't give you goosebumps? Now I want to warm up some vinegar and apple cider vinegar just to see what it's like—you know, compare it to the real thing. Fake pee is outside the scope of my mission statement, but I'm curious by nature and I kind of like the idea. I've always felt a personal kinship and pride in the saying "full of piss and vinegar." I equate it with being a powerful woman.

I've been full of piss and vinegar since the credit card company tried to censor my work. To get credit card processing for anything with sexual content, you have to apply to a high-risk processor. This requires weeks of reviewing bank statements, your website and several forms of government-issued ID, as well as agreeing to exorbitant fees and long-term contracts. It's insane, especially compared to the five minutes it takes to get approved with Stripe or PayPal. Too bad they prohibit adult content. I went through the whole rigmarole and was approved with one caveat. I had to remove all "urine videos" from my website. Problem was, I didn't have any.

I had a spoof on YouTube in which I claimed to be so sexy I pissed glitter, but it's not true. My pee is normal. And that video had no sexual content. It was a YouTube video with ten thousand views and no complaints. My blog is a blog. It started with poetry. Then I posted all my videos on it, both silly YouTube videos and my Masturbation Monday project. It wasn't intended to be an "adult website." It's a woman's website, a woman who is wrestling with serious sexual questions and who also has a sense of humor.

I'd be damned if I was going to pay fifteen hundred dollars, sign a three-year contract, guarantee monthly minimum sales *and* get censored on top of that. Fuck them. I could have removed the pissing-glitter YouTube spoof, but I'd become a righteous ball of anger. Extortion I get. Censorship I get. But to pay extortion rates for censorship pissed me off so bad, I started making piss videos.

I never intended to make any videos with urine until that censorship crap. I often end a bath or shower video with a little experimental footage, but today I'm starting with it. Today it's the central focus, and I'm going to try to make it sexy.

I adjust the overhead camera down a little. I want it to get the piss pooling around my feet and trickling down the drain. Nope. Not a chance. The camera can't see past my boobs. Oh well, facial expressions are important too.

I have no idea how to urinate sexily. This is not part of my social conditioning. It's just baffling. It's also a bit amusing, and something I absolutely have to do. My sense of social justice demands it. I must pee for porn. Fuck censorship, fuck the man.

I'd make a damned high–stakes bet that the guy who handed down the censorship decision was a man who watches porn. I'd also make the same bet for the person writing the policies at the top of the command chain. Most American men watch porn. They just don't admit it, especially if they have a reputation to protect.

The front-view camera is aimed to capture me from navel to knees. The bathroom is too small for a full-body shot. I'm nervous. I don't want to blow my one super-full bladder of the morning on a mediocre shot because I didn't know what would look best. I cross my legs. I open my legs. My curves look best with my legs crossed just slightly. I go with that.

The counter starts on each camera as soon as I press go.

I look straight into the camera and mess my hair up. I rub my hands over the smooth skin of my body. I rock back and forth on my heels. I'm stalling. I strike a demure pose.

I let my bladder go. My piss is the perfect temperature, body temperature. The stream is so forceful, some of it bubbles up, but most of it just runs down my legs. It feels good on my skin. I'm so embarrassed.

I wish I could be getting this from at least four different camera angles. I'm suddenly terrified the piss is a barely visible stream to the cameras' lenses. Cameras aren't always as good as the naked eye.

I open my legs. Urine jettisons from my body, one big stream bouncing off the shower floor and getting all over my feet. I feel like an idiot who couldn't make up her mind, filming half the scene with my legs closed and half the scene with my legs open. I thought maybe the fact that I'm getting it all over myself is what would make it sexy, but maybe it's actually seeing the stream of urine come out that's the sexy part.

The coy look I give the camera is genuinely a mix of emotions.

I'm impressed with myself. I'm still going.

Peeeeeeeee

Peeeeee

Peee

Pee

P

Done.

I rest my hand on the wall. The tiles are cold and shiny, earth tones with gold highlights. Whoa, that was a golden shower, in a golden shower. I make the happiest accidents.

I turn the water on and take my real morning shower, with just a little bit of extra panache. I rub soap in my armpits. It makes a soft fine lather. I rinse and make sure to step in front of the camera casually as the suds run down my tummy.

Peeing didn't get me hot and bothered, at all. That makes sense, but it's a little frustrating for the filming process. I still have to think of something to get myself off.

I was surprised by the credit card processing situation. It's the most tangible slap of sexual shame I've had since childhood. You can earn your way out of other high-risk categories, like car insurance for a new driver by driving responsibly, but there's no way out of the stigma associated with porn.

I used to call my videos erotic short films, but the bots that troll for credit card companies lump all sex on the internet into one big pile of bad. I'm in that pile, just another filthy piss-loving whore. I'm not trying to be better than anyone else. But judgment hurts, especially when you add a sprinkling of injustice and a dollop of the impossible to change. Protesting Mastercard's and Visa's policies on sexually explicit materials seems futile; they're huge, implacable corporations.

I want to open a bank that calculates the risk based on user history, rather than marking entire categories of content high risk, permanently, irrevocably. I should bring a lawsuit. I can just imagine the headline: "Porn Star Sues Visa for Sexual Discrimination." It's not hype. I consider exhibitionist to be my sexual orientation. That's all I need in the midst of divorce. I can just imagine what my soon-to-be-ex-in-laws would say.

One of my biggest fears in making erotic video content is that people will think I'm just doing it for attention, or money.

As if wanting either of those things is bad. Everyone wants attention and money. A good girl just isn't supposed to "use" her sexuality to get it. That's dirty. But I am a good girl, and I like to do bad things.

I'm afraid people will think of me as a nasty urinating miscreant, deriving sexual gratification from perversity or just doing it for the money and attention. In a way it's true. It's always been true. I've only ever used my sexuality for attention, until now. In the privacy of coupling, I handed my sexuality over to men. I had no idea what to do with it myself. I sought his approval, his direction and his attention. Now, I'm making my sexuality public. It is so I have to look at it directly, publicly, witnessed, and confront myself. I am doing this for me more than any other sexual act I've ever engaged in. I couldn't use my sexuality for anything but pleasing others until I started this project. The idea that I can wield it, for my own benefit and pleasure, is the whole point. And I'm still ashamed. I'm sure no one will understand me on this point.

I wet my hair. Water runs over my face. I thought I'd hate the humidity in Florida, but it's been nice. A thin thread of shampoo, the same honey color as my hair, pools in my palm. Fame, money, attention, and sex—these are the forces purported to corrupt a good soul.

I have a dwindling fear that I'll accidentally become someone who actually does things she really didn't want to do, just for money or attention. That I'll become what people expect. I'll listen to their praise or criticism and bend myself accordingly. I'm afraid I'll lose the me I was trying to find before I find her.

It's not an outlandish fear. All my life my sexuality was chained by my need for approval and acceptance, bottled up and labeled "should." I was a good girl. Now I'm a bad girl. I don't care. What I want is to be my own girl. I want to be someone who does what I do because I'm deeply happy.

But I'm scared to trust myself.

I keep these fears in my pocket. I take them out and use them to hone my focus from time to time. My job is to film the truth.

The truth is, I'm pissed.

And in this case, I am doing this *just* for the camera. And with total integrity. I'd never have pissed as part of my "normal" masturbation practice. I did it for the camera, and I did it for the credit card companies. I did it for me. I am cute, coy, blonde, adorable me, hear me roar.

The conditioner rinses out of my hair in a silky sheen down my back. I gotta get my head out of the daydreams and into the moment. I'm clean and wet, and I can't get out of the shower until I orgasm. I close my eyes and think of people watching a thick yellow stream of piss run between my legs. I'm the kind of girl who's that badass, that "fuck you." I'm so punk rock, I'd totally do my laundry with piss if I were stuck in a postapocalyptic hell without manufactured surfactants.

I'm not sure what to do here. I've slipped from thirty percent to twenty percent turned on. I focus in on the sexiest thing in the room, the camera. The camera turns me on. There are definitely things I do just for the camera, and to do them is one hundred percent authentic to my sexuality.

This is taking forever. I have to finish up and get to the convention center. It's networking time. I'm not sure exactly what I'm going to get out of this conference, but masturbating by myself in western Massachusetts isn't going to teach me more about the indie porn world that I've circuitously stepped into.

I give up. I am not going to come in this shower. I grab a towel. I'll have better luck in bed. The room is done in beautiful burgundies, grays and whites. I like this hotel. It's refurbished, 1920s originally, no gym but there are banana trees outside, so what do I care?

I grab a sample of personal lube I picked up at the con yesterday. I rub it on my ass and give the camera a gratuitous view. My back needs moisturizing. I shoot a coy look at the camera. Last, I drip the remaining lube on my clit and close my eyes. My fingers do their circle dance.

I page through the flipbook of my mind: gang rape, gangbang, bad daddy, bad doctor, daddy's friends, another woman, orgy, a specific someone. I imagine every kind of restraint and the people I could be forced to fuck, or let eat my pussy. I could be strapped in the dungeon at the convention, an open oyster bar for any passersby with the munchies (if the dungeon rules allowed for that kind of thing, which they don't). This is a favorite old standby fantasy. The idea of being eaten out by strangers, especially if I can't see them...

My thighs start to quiver. I imagine them strapped open, unable to close. I can buck, fight and scream, but it will do no good.

Oh my God. Jesus Fucking Christ. Yes. Yes. Yes.

I'm half-conscious of my eyes as they roll and flutter. Gaspy maiden-in-distress moans are coming faster. The first contraction sets my boobs a-jiggling. And so does the second. Fantasy is a beautiful thing.

And orgasms are so, so yummy.

Camera Whore is an essay inspired by filming and editing *Pissing in the Rain*, August 2016.

19

ice dragon

"YOU HAVE A SCARY AMOUNT OF ANGER," says my divorce lawyer.

"Really?" I ask, not aware of feeling particularly angry at all. I blink slowly and take a moment with my eyes closed to scan inside myself. The words that surface are "righteous indignation," not "anger." I look at the mild-mannered woman. Her comment seems odd. She's a divorce lawyer. Dealing with angry women is pretty much her job description, isn't it? Maybe she doesn't like her job, or isn't good at it.

Turns out she is totally incompetent. She didn't even get my signature on the right set of divorce papers several months back. The whole process, legally speaking, is starting again from the beginning.

I find a new lawyer.

"You need to do something about your anger," my new divorce lawyer tells me. "It's not healthy." I look at this lawyer with his balding head. The wedding band on his left hand is inscribed with Hebrew. It glints in the light. There are a thousand dismissive statements on the tip of my tongue. A part of me wants to tell him just what a total fucking idiot he is but I

ice dragon

bite it back. I examine a curious fact.

Two divorce lawyers have now told me I have unusual quantities of anger. Divorce lawyers, I assume, see a lot of anger during divorces and know what normal looks like. I wonder if my anger is not just larger than most, but if it is also above average in its caustic qualities.

I resolve to do something about my anger issues.

But I have no idea where to start.

I've been compulsively cheerful my whole life. But the same things that led me to get a divorce also changed my anger-stuffing habit into something else. From the inside I really can't see it. I ask my therapist about how to deal with my anger and receive a photocopied worksheet. On it is a figure something like a gingerbread man or the chalk outline of a homicide scene. The instructions are to record where I feel it in my body when I'm angry. I'm supposed to make Xs over the body parts of the homicide-victim worksheet, and then write a sentence or two describing any sensations I feel.

"Is your anger hot or cold? Is it heavy or explosive?" my therapist asks with a helpful tone that leaves me feeling hopeless. I'd like to take a lighter out of my pocket, burn the worksheet in front of her face, leave its smoldering remains on the carpet, slam the door behind me and peel out on an old motorcycle.

Instead I say thank you, though this worksheet is the stupidest assignment I've received since high school. I don't tell her that. At the end of my appointment, I leave respectfully and drive away in my Prius. I set the worksheets on my desk at home and they disappear, swallowed by a tide of papers.

My anger is creative, changeable and fond of variety, just like the rest of me. One day I am angry and my entire body roils with fire from head to toe. The next day I'm filled with ice-cold dark emptiness that is also somehow angry. But these experiences are either all-encompassing or entirely remote; neither is accessible in any productive way. Describing it leaves me with no greater sense of what it is or where it comes from. I search for latent anger in my calm hours and cannot find it. I believe people. I believe that it's an issue and needs resolving, but when I search for my anger it's just invisible. I knew it's there. Somewhere. But the more I hunt it, the more like a heffalump it becomes. Illusive, threatening and possibly imaginary.

I know I've been angry in the past. I threw a vegetable peeler once. Definitely I was angry then. Happy people don't throw peelers. But the thing is, I can't tell you anything else about the incident. It's a blank. Obviously I was in the kitchen, but was I with my brother or my ex-husband? Was I fifteen or thirty-five? I don't know.

Talking to my therapist seems pointless. Her exercises are a joke. And I have nothing to say about my anger. I know nothing about it. I'd rather work on it myself than get any more of her insipid assignments. I am going to try my own version of art therapy.

I read once that throwing ice cubes in the bathtub was a cathartic approach to anger. The act of hurling something in combination with the din of ice hitting the hard surface was supposedly quite satisfying. I think I'll give it a try. Why not?

After that I could take an ice bath and film it. That would make an interesting masturbation session. The most passionate love scenes were always after a fight, so who knows what accessing anger might stir up in my masturbation practice?

I buy two big bags of ice at the grocery store, and a can of whipped cream for hot cocoa after.

I don a soft blue hat and multicolor scarf that match my bra-and-panty set. It's fun to have something to take off for the camera. I've got the cameras set, the ice bags ready and open.

Okay, time to process my anger.

I feel like an idiot.

I try to find wherever it is inside me that's angry. I don't. I'm half-naked, self-conscious and standing next to embarrassingly large bags of ice in my bathroom.

Oh well. I plunge my hands into the bags and chuck ice into the tub. With a furrowed brow, I try again. My hands are big but the fistfuls of ice seem small. The promised cacophony turns out more like a limp pitter patter. Huh, are the acoustics of my bathtub lacking? I try larger handfuls. No better. Maybe store-bought ice cubes are too soft. I grab the tray of ice from my freezer. No improvement. My hands get cold. This isn't fun. Or helpful. Or satisfying. Each piece of ice is small and inconsequential. And I feel so ridiculous I can't help but smile like a goon.

True smiles chase away anger. When happy is your default setting, "processing anger" is a puzzling conundrum. The harder I throw, the more weak and pathetic my efforts feel. I give up. Ice cube hucking is not going to do it for me.

I pop an ice cube in my mouth and drool seductively. I breathe through the hole at the center of the ice. Melt and saliva drip. I suck and blow, reveling in the moment. I'm back in my element now that I'm aiming at sexy rather than angry. The cylindrical ice cube fits the "o" of my mouth perfectly, which means it isn't a cube at all.

I flirt shamelessly and make eyes at the camera.

Ice is cold. Hands, lips and tongue are cold.

I'm not looking forward to this polar bath.

I empty ten pounds of ice into the tub and turn the cold tap. Maybe the hidden flames of my anger will drown in an ice bath. I could be a soaked dragon, impotently spewing smoke.

I hop into the tub. Ice water swirls around my calves. I shriek. I want to jump back out immediately but I stand there and shiver as I count aloud. I must stay in the water for at least twenty seconds.

"Seventeen, eighteen, nineteen, twenty." For good measure I add, "Twenty-one, twenty-two."

I jump out, dance about on the bath mat a few moments.

I force myself back in quickly.

"Nine, ten, eleven."

I do it again. And again, until the cold doesn't feel so cold.

For a real ice bath, I need to submerge. I'm working up to it. I sit. Ice cubes bump against my waist. I emit constricted panting noises, fists waving about. My parasympathetic nervous system tells me to run, but my will dictates I stay put. The collision of these parts of my mind result in the huffing and puffing of cheeks, and head-to-toe trembling.

I'm doubtful all this hubbub will extinguish the hidden inferno inside me. I'm certain my rage is rolling its distant eyes at all this preposterousness. It will not be exorcised by such undignified means.

Jesus Effing Christ. I give up. Time to masturbate. I won't orgasm in this ice bath before hypothermia sets in. I refill the tub with hot water. If one can't extinguish one's rage, the next best thing is to blow off some sexual tension in a nice warm tub.

The traditional antidote to a plunge in ice water is a spell in the sauna. I don't have a sauna but I do have a cup of hot cocoa, a scalding-hot bath and a good attitude.

Oh, and I have a can of whipped cream.

Happiness, thy name is whipped cream. Under a cap of sweet fluff, I sip hot cocoa. It's soft and slurpy. Warm, sweet goodness. Yum, yum. I lick it from the edges of my lips.

I lie back in the tub, close my eyes and rub.

I need to think of something super naughty, or super sexy, or super loving. Loving thoughts make me sad and lonely too often. Naughty it is, then. What bad things can I think of? Polar bear bestiality? No. Um, maybe something opposite, like girls on the beach in bikinis? No, boring. I'm not going to think of anything good. I float and watch my boobs wobble. As goofy as they are, I really am glad to have them. They are cozy.

I take another sip of cocoa. It needs more whipped cream. I give it a generous swirly squirt and set the can of whipped cream back on the bathroom windowsill. Sipping hot cocoa in a hot bath is really quite a luxury.

I look at the can of whipped cream, and it looks back at me. I feel ambushed.

I don't mean to but I decide to put whipped cream on my hoo-ha.

"Decide" is not the right word.

It's like I know, suddenly, that the whipped cream is the secret key, the thing that will get me off. "Decide" sounds like I chose the whipped cream, but it chose me. I thought I was buying the whipped cream for the cocoa, but all along it knew it was coming for me. Deep certainty settles in me, and I don't really like it. It's a horrible idea. It could stir up a yeast infection. And besides, who puts whipped cream on their hoo-ha?

Really. I'm forty. I'm too old for pranks like this. Except that apparently I am not.

The whipped cream ending is inevitable, and probably predictable to everyone but me. I should have known if I took a bath with hot cocoa, of course it would come to this. I shake my head.

With resignation and mirth, I grab the can from the windowsill again.

There is something exciting about aerosol propulsion.

The can is weighty in my hand, bottom heavy. I tip and shake. Pelvis up, legs akimbo, I press the nozzle to the side and cool piles of frilly dairy coat my pubic area. I reach my fingers in and start working it. My God. I can't believe I'm doing this. Neither can the whipped cream. It melts and slides rather fast. I get another squirt on my clit and cover my parts.

I focus. I feel. I think only of the situation I'm in, and that it will be witnessed.

The cream is cold. Reaching into it is slick and thick. I rub fast.

Orgasm, come here orgasm, quick before it melts.

My eyes blink open. My pussy is a white mound of froth, like the mouth of a rabid dog. I imagine a kinky submissive cleaning me up with his tongue.

Fuck.

A wave of energy spills over me, the crest breaking over my head and the rest crashing through my body. Naughtiness and a nip of mortification is all it takes to tip me over the edge into the delights of orgasm. I do not understand myself, but I am grateful to be me.

I lower my hips into the bath, watching the whipped cream

float away and dissipate. I may have scary amounts of anger, but until I figure out what to do about it, I decide orgasms are a fine way to knock the edge off.

Ice Dragon is an essay inspired by filming and editing *Anger Management on Ice*, October 2016.

20

teabagging

MY NOSE IS RAW FROM BLOWING. My eyes are glassy and my bed is shrouded in used tissues. I'm sick and it's time for the weekly masturbation practice. This is a challenge to my theory that anything can be sexy. I want to believe you can be sexy even when you feel unlovable, shy, ugly, skinny, fat, flatulent or sick. I'm suffused with doubt, but I'm going to try anyway. I've been trying to prove to myself that sexy isn't an outside label but an inside state of affairs. I blow my nose. This will be quite a test.

I observe the situation and meditate for a moment on staying connected to my authenticity, though that overhyped word makes me a little queasy. Even if I film today, I need to take care of myself. That means tea, soup and rest. No Nyquil and faking sexy. I'm going to be true to being sick.

Wait.

Am I going to blow my nose in a porno?

What a ghastly idea.

I have to do it.

My snot maker is overactive even when I'm not sick. There is a no-percent chance that I won't have to blow my nose while filming. I'm excited. I might not edit out all my schnozzle honking. It's a small taboo but still it makes me catch my breath. Can I be that free? Can I blow my nose in a porno and still be loved, or at least not ridiculed?

I take my flannel-jammied ass to the kitchen and film the making of tea and the heating of soup. I'm in artsy mode and enjoy the minutiae. Water splashes the interior glass of my electric teapot. Light shines through the turbulent bubbly water. I turn the tap off. The water settles into serenity so fast it's startling. I swipe the camera into slo-mo and ignite the gas burner under the soup. I love fire. I don't watch the teapot, but my camera does, and eventually it boils. The tea pouch tears easily. I drop the useless wrapper on the counter and marvel at the raw destructive power in my fingertips.

By reputation, herbal tea is mild mannered, healthy and comforting. Don't be fooled. Boiling water is required to make tea do its infusey thing and let the yumminess out. Boiling water is violent, dangerous and beautiful. Tea is dangerous while becoming itself. It's that very hotness, the lingering of its recently threatening state, that makes it the most comforting. Woah, I can see rabbit holes of metaphysical parallels to kink. This tea drinking is a deep experience.

I'm a tea drinker all the time, but usually I'm too busy to manage more than a sip or two while it's still warm. I've developed a taste for tea at any temperature from tepid to rather cold. But being sick stops the world. And I indulge in the rare luxury of drinking tea while it's still hot. The heat of the tea transfers to the ceramic clay of the mug. The water's heat becomes the mug's heat becomes my hand's heat becomes deep joy. I put my stuffy nose over the steam. There's nothing else I have to do but get this glorious warm liquid down my gullet while it's still warm.

Simple. Pleasure.

In my mind, hot liquid melts the stuffiness from my ears and nose. Even partial relief from the discomfort of congestion feels wonderful. Reclaiming ease I take for granted on a healthy day is a gift that yields genuine gratitude. I am a tea lover.

I am also an amateur porn producer and a lover of words. I know what perversions true tea lovers might get themselves up to. I learned about teabagging from summer camp stories in the eighties. The knowledge has remained academic and a wee bit vague. I've sucked balls. I love sucking balls. But with all the scrotum joy I've experienced, I don't think anyone has ever dipped in and out of my mouth in a manner I'd call teabagging.

I can teabag this tea bag though, I think with a mischievous glint in my eye.

I let the tea bag drip little drops on my chin. The bag spins on its string. It's messy. I laugh and giggle. I am sick and I feel alive. The warm dribbles on my chin turn cold. Sip, dip, lick and flick, I do tea bag tricks with my tongue. The conceit is working. I never thought a cup of Throat Coat tea would be sexy, but it is.

I blow my nose and look at the camera, as if in submission, as if embarrassed to let these parts of me show. With my eyes I say, *find me beautiful and lovable anyway.* And I kinda am. I throw the tissue in the trash and flop back in bed.

Sucking a tea bag and attempting to sexily blow my nose is ridiculous. Sex is ridiculous, being human is ridiculous. I am ridiculous. And wonderful. But there is no amount of sucking tea bags that is going to make me orgasm. Foreplay alone does not a masturbation practice make.

I don't actually know how to be sexy while I'm sick. I think about what might turn me on and give up quickly. Fuck this, I need sustenance.

I bring a bowl of homemade chicken soup back to bed. There is no way I can make slurping soup sexy. Pictures of people eating are notoriously unflattering. It's on the no-no list for photography. Just don't do it. I eat the bowl of soup. I know it's not sexy. I don't even try to make it sexy. It's nourishing. Nourishing is good. Malnourishment is not sexy.

Does that mean I've tangentially furthered the sexiness cause?

I'm thinking too much.

I lick the bowl. Long slow tongue strokes inside its smooth curves. Naughty girl. I stare into the camera with big blue eyes. It's a cheap shot, but licking is always sexy, even when it's chicken noodle soup.

I'm getting excited now, but nowhere near orgasm.

I will actually have to stimulate my clitoris. Sigh. I'm tired. I'm sick. I'm a lazy ass for good reason today. If there was any day for guilt-free use of a Hitachi, it's today.

I grab my Japanese orgasm maker and get back in bed. I love being in bed. I love the fluffiness of pillows and comforters. My breasts are so naked under my flannel jammies. It's titillating. My silly feet are hidden in thick wool socks. I dance them around seductively and tease the camera with my legs. I unbutton the pajamas deliberately and relish revealing my breasts. They are beautiful today. My hips move in small circles, slowly. My jammies are purple with green dinosaurs and hula dancers.

I press the bulbous vibrating end of the Hitachi to my nipple. It is buzzy. Really buzzy. The electric bliss trails lower until the head chatters over my clit through the soft cloth of my jammies and panties. I keep it there, waking my baser hungers. I repose half under the duvet, eyes closed, feeling.

I remove my pajama bottoms with a flourish and get the buzzy head right on my clit and opening. Wet sounds join the vibrating noise as my hips rock up and down, seeking pleasure. I imagine I'm not alone. My mouth opens in arousal and my hips grow bold, jutting up and down with rigor.

I am humping my Hitachi.

My eyes roll back and convulsions take my body.

Hitachi orgasms aren't usually my best orgasms, they tend to be fast and dry, but I'm not complaining. I'd never heard of a Hitachi before this summer. A cam model I filmed with in Florida talked me into buying this one. Conventions are for learning the tricks of a trade.

I keep the Hitachi on my clit. It's almost painful on the heels of orgasm. I've got nothing better to do, so I switch from a steady hum to one of the Hitachi's pre-programmed modes. I wiggle and squirm. I mewl with agony and pleasure. My legs tremble. I orgasm again, a smaller one but impressive for being a doubleheader.

I'm done for now.

I try to balance the Hitachi on my face, and fail. I like the way it smells of me. I'm happy. I've made a beautiful video while in bed sick and alone. I've got the warm glow of orgasm in my belly. Once I get the cameras turned off, I'm going to nap. I've earned it.

Teabagging is an essay inspired by filming and editing *Sick Day*, November 2016.

21

traffic jam

"I NEED TO PICK UP FLOORING," I tell my boyfriend.

"I'll drive you," he offers.

My new boyfriend is so handsome it makes me blush. Now that I'm legally unwed, I'm totally over being single. The ink has had three months to dry on my divorce papers. Since they were signed, all kinds of things have been freed up, from sex to renovations. The apartment my ex and I were remodeling was hogtied for over a year in the bureaucracy of the divorce.

I'm anxious to get it finished and rented. I need the money.

Need is a brilliant force that makes my creative juices extra slick and juicy. I need to make a masturbation video, and I need to remodel my apartment. I review the ingredients on hand for today's film: a pussy, a car, an errand, a driver and a deadline. What is the best short film I can make with these props, in this situation? The questions are like a competition. How much wacky inspiration can I draw from life? Can I top the film I made last week?

I did a film two months ago, where I painted the trim in the upstairs apartment with long sexy brush strokes and lots of cleavage, before devolving into something akin to twerking. It was really embarrassing, but my fans still seemed to love it. Making a day repainting old trim into sexy porn is my kind of challenge.

I like the restrictions and limitations. I like something to push against. It makes me bold. I straddle deadlines like a bull rider, focused and tenacious in the face of danger.

I throw on thigh highs and a silk skirt, grab my camera gear and get in the car. It's a sunny December afternoon. My boyfriend and I are all full of smiles. Everything is going to be perfect.

I place one camera on the floor for an upskirt shot. The other camera starts on the visor, getting a bird's-eye view. I make a show of straightening my skirts and taking off my gloves. I move the camera to the dashboard for face shots.

Traffic slows.

This is rare in Western Massachusetts. We don't really have traffic, and yet traffic comes almost to a stop. I look around in furtive gratitude. Extra time to reach climax is a boon, the universe smiling a favor on me. But traveling at five miles per hour, I grow self-conscious of what others might see. I rub my clit discreetly, pulling my panties aside rather than off. Fingers explore, stroking soft creases, flicking my clit and stretching my labia. Outside. Inside. Open. Close. I keep my skirts pulled over my knees so even a passing trucker couldn't see much.

I'm wearing plain lavender cotton panties. Part of me cringes to be wearing such unsexy underwear. The other part of me says they're a nice accent, unpretentious and wafting innocence. My fingers perform their wanton flirtations for the camera, petting my pussy lips. My head rests against the window. I try to let thoughts read across my face. *I'm bored with nothing else to do.*

traffic jam

Don't mind me, I'll just toy with my privates in the car as I wait. I think these thoughts as loud as I can and hope they translate into some interesting facial expressions. The window is cold on my cheek. I play with the ribbon at the top of my thigh highs.

We pass the accident that caused the slowdown. I'm touching myself with police lights flashing behind me; it doesn't get much better than this. I keep rubbing myself on the down-low, my legs open just a little. I try not to be gleeful at how awesome the footage is going to be. I love doing naughty things under the nose of authority. I scold myself. This car accident is someone else's rough day. The scolding does little to dampen my elation.

As the flashing lights fade behind us, I hope it's not a tragic day for those in the accident.

The speedometer climbs and I grow bold.

I take my panties off.

We hit seventy.

I don't have much time left, eight more minutes or so on the freeway. I need to orgasm. I need to get off before we get off. I can't orgasm at an intersection in small-town America. It just isn't right. And it will be too dark to film on the way home. I close my eyes tight and rub like mad.

I open my knees and place my feet wide on the dashboard in a position similar to the stirrups at a gynecological exam. My hand tightens around the safety harness across my chest.

I let every possible scenario flit through my mind—threesomes, infidelity, denial, humiliation. Nah, this situation is enough. I focus on my compromised position, my vulnerability, how exposed I am, to the camera, to my boyfriend, to the future audience of the film, to another car if it was a super-high rider. I rub faster. The sign says one mile to the exit.

Holy fuck, I have to make this happen. My body is warm in the right way. I'm glowing, it's growing dark, the car rumbles along, fast. My boyfriend is quiet, letting me focus on my work. I have to orgasm. Now. I close my eyes.

To my shock and eternal gratitude, I birth a gigantic orgasm.

I can't believe it. If I weren't strapped into the car with a safety belt, I'd be doing cartwheels, my bare pussy smiling at the sky. The orgasm aftershocks subside and the engine slows for the off-ramp. The sound of the engine decelerating is perfectly timed.

I keep the camera rolling and lick my fingers clean, one by one.

Yum, pussy juice.

Traffic Jam is an essay inspired by filming and editing *Nailed & Painted*, September 2016; and *Traffic Jam*, December 2016.

22

lost

MY BOYFRIEND PISSED ME OFF AGAIN, I text Erin.

Want a girl's night Friday? she offers. *I can drive up.*

I'm going to Providence, without him now I think. Want to do a girl's night out there? You are welcome to join me for the kink conference Saturday, or not.

Tempting! I'm not too impressed with my boyfriend right now either. Where are you planning to stay? Erin asks.

I'm debating between a gorgeous hotel with a sauna and riverfront view for $165. It's a very modern and sleek rehab of an old mill building. The other option is a shared private room at a youth hostel for $80, spare and minimal with shared bathrooms. I'm tempted to indulge. Thoughts?

Let's do it. You had me at 'sauna'!

I'll make the reservation. See you tomorrow, so excited!

I pack with bated breath. My boyfriend could walk in the door any minute. He hasn't mentioned anything about our weekend trip in over a week. I'm going to this kink conference to educate myself about the sex-positive community at large. It's a business trip, but my business is pleasure right now. I thought he could benefit from the discussions on consent. He self-identifies as "naturally dominant." So did the two lovers I had during the open phase at the end of my marriage. I'm beginning to equate the phrase with unexamined entitlement, disrespect and manipulation.

I throw fishnets, whips, heels, pajamas, lube and condoms in a suitcase. I'm packing fast, but part of me hopes he'll get home from work before I leave. I want him to come with me. I want him to learn better boundaries and communication skills. I want it to work with us. But he so doesn't deserve to ride my coattails at this conference, not after the way he's treated me this week. This past few weeks.

At 5:01, I'm in the car. I set the coordinates and text Erin.
I won't be there until almost seven, just leaving now.
I'll be there by eight, she answers.

Midday Erin gets cold feet about coming, but she's coming. I'm so glad. It sucks to be going alone. I'm anxious and miserable.

I'll need a video to post on Sunday. I could film while I drive. The in-car masturbation video I made recently was not the way I really masturbate in the car. Usually I'm not chauffeured about. Like airplane masturbation, car masturbation was one of the few ways I masturbated before this experiment. Maybe there's something about travel. Maybe cars and planes travel faster than the speed of shame. Maybe it's the boredom that you can't escape, maybe it's the enclosed space, maybe it's the stir of change.

I should make a video now.

Oh my God, that would give viewers a heart attack. They won't be able to get off to my video because they'll be too scared

I'm going to end up a bloody smear on the windshield. Not all dicks and clits wither at the sight of blood, I muse.

Shut up, I tell myself. This isn't about how the audience might or might not jack shit. This is a documentary of sorts, and research. I've masturbated while driving. It's a fact. It's a notable fact, even if it's a super-horrible thing. I feel obliged to be honest about it.

I grab my Hitachi and make a silent promise that I'll film without looking, my eyes won't leave the road. The camera will catch what it will. Safety first.

Damn.

I hold the camera facing out and catch a bit of scenery. I get the freeway signs as I pass underneath. The street lights grow bright as the night grows dark. I switch the camera to face my lap and record the Hitachi buzzing away between my thighs.

Careful, stay focused on the road, just let the camera get what the camera gets. The Hitachi is loud, so loud. It feels good. It's been a few days since it snowed, the roads are clear and dry.

"Exit 43 onto Route 1," Siri says.

Damn, I was going to come. I check the rearview and change lanes with care. It's turn and exit, turn and exit. I can't get back to that fuzzy warm about-to-boil feeling. I can barely get a simmer on with all the lane changes and high-maintenance driving.

There is something very wrong. I'm supposed to be going into a city but I'm on a fucking dirt road. The Hitachi is holding steady between my legs. My phone screen says the hotel is three minutes away. I'm on a dirt fucking road, in the dark, alone, no panties on, rumbling slowly through the unknown.

An old factory looms up in the dark and I hump up and over the transition to a paved road. Thank God.

"Arrived…"

Orgasm rolls over me. Between shuddering contractions, a speed limit sign flashes by. Five miles per hour, it says.

"…destination, Providence," Siri announces.

My speed and timing are spot fucking on. I'm amazeballs, without even trying.

I park the car across the street from the hotel. I'm impressed; the refurbishments look great from here. But I don't want to get out of the car. It's cold. It's February cold, unforgiving and vindictive. I'm alone. Maybe I'll hang out until Erin arrives, then we can go in together. I can stay here and keep filming until then.

I don't technically need masturbation videos anymore. I hit the one-year mark almost two months ago. But I keep filming and posting because what else am I going to post on my blog? And my subscribers expect it. According to the terms I wrote on my subscription page, funds support all my work, YouTube, writing and blogging. But my fans have made it clear that they expect a weekly video on my blog. All the marketing books say to keep expectations simple and clear; branding should be the same.

I am not a simple girl.

I need to write my book. I should be spending the time I'm spending making films, writing. That's what the whole project is for, research into my sexuality. Now it's time to make sense of it all. What have I learned this year?

Nothing.

That's the big gaping hole of an answer in my chest.

I don't know what to do with the expectations of the audience I've built. They want the videos to continue. And I don't know what to do with this pit of sorrow where my boyfriend should be.

I should go check in. It's creepy to sit in a parking lot, alone in the dark. I stare at the hotel across the street.

I don't want to get out of the car.

I lean back, turn the Hitachi on again and pull my shirt up, exposing my breasts to the shadows of the night.

The second orgasm is louder, and closing my eyes for this one is a luxury.

I extract myself from the car. I'm wishing I was inside already before I can even wrestle the suitcase out of the back seat. It is cold. I head toward the hotel. Will the salt on the sidewalk ruin the wheels on my suitcase, I wonder. My phone rings.

"Hi, it's Erin. I'm so sorry. I just can't make it tonight."

My fingers are cold. It's windy. I'm standing alone in the dark at the edge of the parking lot on an icy sidewalk, so I can fucking listen to her stand me up. I end the call as quickly as possible. I should have asked her to chip in for the hotel anyway, 'cause I'd be at the hostel in dorm-style accommodations for forty dollars if she hadn't said yes, but I don't have the energy to ask.

This is my first time staying in a hotel that calls itself "boutique." The shower walls are curved glass that bumps into the bedroom area, giving whomever a perfect silhouette. In this case whomever is no one. A few days ago my boyfriend went to visit his ex-girlfriend for a few hours but "accidentally" fell asleep and stayed all night.

I didn't disinvite him from this weekend. I just didn't bother to remind him either. In the days before I left, he didn't appear to remember. I slipped away for the weekend without a word.

Being alone in this hotel room is my reward, and punishment.

I struggle to sleep.

My suitcase is a shambles of who knows what, packed with a broken heart and a muddled mind. I'm disgusted at the drama distracting me. I'm here to figure out how to share my work with a wider audience and help people shed their shame too. The fishnets sproing out of my suitcase, like rubber bands snagged on my stilettos. I can't wear them. I can't wear anything sexy. I'm not sexy, I'm a ball of pain. *It's okay,* I tell myself. I'm not dressing to impress, or even to participate. No latex, no pasties, just a simple black dress and a pair of pearl earrings.

I'm here to network.

The breakfast buffet is delicious but overpriced. I can't eat enough to get my value. I pocket a few extra tea packets. I won't be ripped off.

The conference is a short drive away, but it's only grown colder and windier. The conference parking lot is full to the edges. I'll be hoofing it in heels. It's biting cold. It's butt-fucking cold. How appropriate for kinksters and fetishists.

There'll be no biting or butt fucking for me this weekend, I think as I follow behind someone wearing rainbow sparkle platform heels, a collar with a leash, a bodysuit and a spiky wig. I don't know if he's a cross-dresser, they are genderfluid, or she is a trans woman. Regardless, the costume and its wearer look damn fine in all that glitter and glam. I wish I was in the mood to wear something like that. The outfit screams, *Look at me. I am fabulousness incarnate and I'm not afraid to sparkle and shine.*

That's how I should be.

I've wanted to come to this event for years, but usually I'm with my daughter and ex at a family dance weekend. It's his custody this week, and I'm free to be here guilt free. I should be having fun. The cold wind bites through me. I'm finally here and I'm in no mood to enjoy it.

I follow the flow of people through the large glass hotel doors and pay my twenty-five dollars.

"We just have to put a sticker over the camera lens," the people at check-in tell me.

With reluctance I hand my iPhone over. I do it for the health of the community, like vaccines, but I don't like it. There is going to be so much amazing stuff, and all of it should be posted to my social media. But if privacy wasn't taken seriously, no one would come to these events.

"Sarah?!?!?" I say. I can't believe I just walked into her booth. I'd just been thinking that I needed to email that nice woman I met in Florida. Sarah Gregory, the spanking queen. She has a whole room just for her DVDs and favorite spanking implements.

"How are you?" I ask. She answers but I'm a bit too overwhelmed to follow.

"Will you shoot with me?" she asks.

I'm floored. I've been plotting since August to ask her to let me be in one of her videos. Before I even have a chance to work up to it, she asks me!

"You can top, right?"

"Absolutely," I say. I just topped in a video for the first time last month. I didn't have a fucking clue what I was doing, but it was fun. And with a background in massage and dance I've got body awareness. Besides, I've been a bottom, I can build from what I know I like in a top. That's enough experience, right? Oh, God. I'm so fucking in over my head. I'll find some asses to practice on between now and whatever shoot we schedule. I wish they had self-help audiobooks on BDSM. I don't have time to read real books.

I say my good-byes and wander down the hall. Each room on the first floor has become a a BDSM boutique. It's like an indoor fetish mall. I enter a room with gleaming wooden beams in sturdy configuration. I have never been chained to a St. Andrew's cross but the craftsmanship is a marvel. It makes me drool. The woodworking is superb. I want to try it out. I want to be restrained.

"This flogger is made of recycled lumber. The wood comes from old church pews."

My panties get wet at the idea of using this repurposed religious relic. I have to have it.

In the privacy of the hotel rooms, with permission of the vendor, you can snap a shot, supposedly. I do. I get one of me wearing a black leather blindfold with the word "slut" embossed in pink letters, and one of me riding a toy rocking horse with rideable moving dildo. I snap a few of some amazing ball-crunching devices too.

My boyfriend loves it when I squeeze his balls. I'm "deadlifts one hundred and eighty pounds" strong, but I can't grip hard enough for him no matter how I try. These ball crushers are finely made. I'd love to watch him inspect the quality of the machining. The thought of sliding the cold steel over his ball sack makes me quiver. The gleaming of the metal would contrast with his dark skin. Maybe he wouldn't like metal. Maybe he's only into the warm grasp of a woman's fist.

I send him a picture, just to make him wish he was here.

God, I wish he was here. He's such an idiot. I am a dream come true. I like threesomes, I'm adventurous, I clean, I cook, I'm nice to children. And he doesn't seem to value me at all. Fuck.

Looks like you are having fun, baby.

His text pulls the knife out of my heart. I sigh. I wish I wasn't smiling so big, but I am. I love him.

I watch a flogging demo by Midori. She's like a master dancer. She talks of oceans and poetry as her flogger caresses every curve of a large man's back, groin and chest. She makes us laugh but her authority and control don't waver. There's not an ounce of bullshit or bluster in this tiny woman, just love of what's she's doing. She commands the largest crowd I see all weekend, and makes it look effortless. I want to be Midori.

People with ponytails attached to their asses pull chariots down the hall. They're covered in black latex from head to toe. I wish they had coconuts to make the clip-clop sound like in *Monty Python and the Holy Grail.*

This place is certainly some kind of holy grail. After seven hours, I'm exhausted.

I head back to my hotel. And my empty bed.

I want the oblivion of sleep. Blot the pain, please. I toss and turn.

Sun streams in the window over the bed. A creek sparkles and shines like fool's gold. I've got two hours to film and get out the door. Decent timing: I usually take an hour to film and an hour to dress.

One camera goes on the back of the toilet and the other next to the bed. I'll be getting a full body shot and a simultaneous silhouette. It's going to be so cool! I'm a happy little nut right now. I'm going to have two masturbation videos to go home with. I like being ahead a week or two in footage. It's good in case of emergencies. Or if I ever want a vacation. It would be good to take a week or two off. As if.

The cameras roll and I start with brushing my hair. Fans have asked for hair brushing, and ASMR. Google says ASMR stands for Autonomous Sensory Meridian Response. Sounds like New Age bullshit, but from what I can tell in other videos it's a fetish for pretty girls who whisper and make relaxing noises. For the most part I ignore fan requests. This work is about pursuing this woman's conception of female pleasure. There's enough portraits out there of women pleasing men…but since I have to brush my hair anyway, I go ahead and film it.

I play peekaboo in the shower curtain. Water pours out of the huge round showerhead. I run my fingers through my hair as I wet it, my elbows in the air. I exaggerate the movement and arch my back. It's going to look amazing. I jut my tits into the spray of water. My butt pops out in the universal mammalian "mount me" signal. The postures of sex appeal are turning me on. I wash my hair and am crazy generous with the conditioner. I make crazy faces at the camera while I work it into my hair. I rub my clit as water streams down my body.

I try the handheld shower nozzle between my legs. It looks good. Water arcs up, front then back. It tickles my ass. My pussy doesn't like it, but my ass does. I want to come.

Urban legend has it that a toothbrush makes a good sex toy. I don't come, not even with a toothbrush.

Not much makes a girl feel stupider than standing in a shower with a toothbrush on her clit and failing to orgasm. I sit down. From down here the shower is like rain. Sitting on the shower floor with a toothbrush on my clit and failing to orgasm is worse.

I crawl into bed still damp. It will be easier to orgasm in bed where my natural lubes aren't being rinsed away. I rub and rub.

I try not to think about my boyfriend. His absence is a knife in my chest. I try not to wish he'd text me. I tuck the white fluffy pillows under me from at least three different angles, searching for the sexy. I close my eyes and think of every hot thing I can imagine. What if I was blindfolded, gangbanged? What if I had two men at the same time?

Nothing.

Fruitless.

Failure.

A year of dedication to a "masturbation practice" and I still can't have a fucking orgasm when I want one. I'd keep at it. I'd make myself orgasm, Goddammit, but checkout is in less than ten minutes. They already turned down my request for a late checkout.

It's time to go. I should drive west, but I don't want to go home. My boyfriend is bad for me. It's not just the shit he's pulled in the last few weeks. He's been nothing but half-truths and manipulations since the day we met. I close my eyes and grip the steering wheel. I gave him his first threesome this month. A few days later he didn't give me a Valentine's Day gift, just a card that said I made him horny. That's the least of his crimes, but it hurts. I thought I meant something to him. God, I wish I didn't miss him so bad it's physical. I crave him.

After checking out, I wrack my brain for somewhere to go. I need time. I need food. I stop for Thai food and order chicken green coconut curry. The chicken is moist and tender, thin slices drenched in sweet coconut with pepper and basil. It's so good I lick the plate.

I know going home is a bad idea. I'm intoxicated by his charm and his sex appeal and his super cuddling powers. He clouds my mind.

Again I ask myself where else I could go. Emmy pops into mind. *Hey, chica, want surprise company? I'm volunteering to couch surf at your place,* I text her.

Yes! Where are you? When will you arrive?

I'm two and a half hours away, I text as a wave of relief crashes over me.

I'm working, but if you don't mind being on your own some, it would be great to see you!

I wipe a half tear from my eye and turn north. In a few hours I'll be in a safe place where people love me. And I'll be able to think. And I'll start writing.

I sit in bed with my sexy silver laptop for hours at a time. Emmy's husband is an artist. Their home is striking. Emmy works from home. We break for healthy meals together but work in peaceable silence in adjacent rooms all morning and all afternoon. In the evening they tell me I deserve better. This guy isn't treating me right. They insist I should stay as long as I want. I'm so lucky to have friends like these. I tell them so, and I tear up.

The longer I stay, the clearer my vision gets. I stay for days. My boyfriend texts. He asks when I'm coming home. He says he misses me. He sounds apologetic, but I know better. I knew from the first time he took my car without asking and took another woman on a date with it and didn't even fill the tank.

He uses me.

I drive home determined to tell him to move out. I've asked before, but this time I'm giving him thirty days' notice, in writing.

Lost is an essay inspired by filming and editing *Providence* and *Frosted Shower with Toothbrush*, February 2017.

23

i need therapy

THE WORDS STICK IN MY THROAT. The blood rushes to my cheeks. I'm dying of mortification. I know these words sounded good when I wrote them, but they're horrible now.

"Here, you read it," I say and shove my laptop at Maggie.

She graciously reads,

"On occasion I dress like a young girl in a sexually provocative way. Good women don't do that. Making a film that fessed up to this part of my sexuality was scary. I expected my work to meet with derision for my daddy issues, disgust at filming in public and worst of all, accusations of promoting pedophilia. I quivered a little at a mountain of judgments, packed my film equipment in my backpack and walked up to the park near my house at dawn, when all the good little boys and girls were still abed and I could film in public without involving the public. I imagined what early risers in the neighborhood were thinking of a woman with her hair in two braids with satin bows, wearing a pink square-dancing dress."

It's horrible. I hate it. I swear it was good when I wrote it. I don't know what happened in the past few months while

I finished the manuscript. I've got twenty thousand words of free write. Now I need a book, not this shit. I can't start over. It's already taken more than two months to write, evenings, weekends and all of spring break.

Summer vacation begins. I can focus one hundred percent on my manuscript.

I get even less editing done.

Every time I sit at my computer, I'm besieged with nausea. Stomach cramps follow. I sit hunched in misery.

What if I can't write this book? What if I spent over a year collecting research footage for a book I can't write? I collected thousands of names on my mailing list with the promise of a book that I'm afraid I'll never finish.

I can't flake out.

I have to write this book.

I will never respect myself again if I don't.

"Switching between the first-person narrative and the academic tone is a bit jarring," Maggie says.

It's a useful insight.

"Thank you," I say.

I mean it. She's right. It's a problem I can fix.

In the days that come, I split the essay in two. One is written in the first person. I decide this one is written by Jupiter's Slut, the part of me that doesn't justify herself. The other is an analysis of my fears and a justification of my work. I decide that is written by Jupiter, my intellectual part.

I start editing the next essay.

I can't do it. I can't even read it. I sit there and stare at the screen. Nausea grips me until I'm shaking.

I tell myself that I can't do anything else until I get this essay edited.

I sit for hours, and nothing happens.

I'm losing my shit.

I'm afraid this depression is making me a bad mom. I find myself snapping at my daughter. I'm aloof. I don't mean to absent but I haven't heard a word she's said.

I set goals and deadlines; those worked during the filming. They don't work now. I try forcing myself with accountability check-ins on a new YouTube channel. For a few weeks I report on writing goals.

The videos won't upload, and one gets flagged for deletion. That's a strike against my account. I was fully clothed, only talking. I didn't even mime sex acts. YouTube's community reporting gives too much power to anonymous dweebs. I didn't break the rules. Not even close. I appeal the strike. Nothing is rectified. I can't put energy into another channel that might get deleted.

Fuckers.

I need the book finished before I have to go back to teaching in the fall.

Oh my God, what if I'm just like my dad? Dread tightens my chest. Am I a dreamer, a never-doer? Is this self-sabotage? I want to scream.

I can't wish and wonder for the rest of my life.

Day after day I sit until it's clear that the more I sit the more my life falls apart. My mind is ratcheting and if I let it go any further I'm going to strip my threads.

They say "butt in chair" is the secret to a writer's success. My life grinds to a halt, like bones in an old stone mill.

"Well," I say to myself, "we are going to try another strategy.

You are going to do whatever you *can* do. If that's simply wash the dishes, that's what you'll do."

I wash the dishes. I wash a lot of dishes. I walk.

I listen to self-help audiobooks all day. Listening to someone else say something positive, anything positive, is better than listening to myself.

I work on it with my counselor.

"I'm terrified what my neighbors will think," I say.

"Tell me about it," she prompts.

"It's just a big black void," I tell her.

She uses Eye Movement Desensitization and Reprocessing with me, EMDR for short. It calms me some but I don't understand what I'm so scared of.

I cry.

I cry harder.

I cry a lot.

I go to conferences. The same ones as last year, when I was just starting out, but this time I'm greeted as a friend. I remember how scary it was to walk into a sea of sex advocates, sex educators and sex workers last year, not knowing a soul. On the last night of one of my favorite events, I go on stage in pigtails and fishnets, whining like a five-year-old that I just want cock. The audience doesn't breathe. I can feel it.

They don't know what to make of me. I tell them I'm lucky, really, really lucky, because some of my friends are sex geeks, and they've helped me dream bigger dreams than I ever dreamed of dreaming. The friends I've planted in the audience join me on stage, their strap-on dicks bouncing glorious and free. I speed-suck the strap-ons.

The applause is uproarious.

I go back to the shrink when I get home.

I'm afraid people will think I'm promoting pedophilia, that I hate God and that I'm hurting society. A friend gives me a private session of Emotional Freedom Techniques, or EFT.

"I'm scared and I love me just the way I am," I say.

I feel like an idiot tapping my energy points. I'd rather be mocking these techniques than using them.

My first YouTube video was teasing self-help bullshit like this. I lightly spoofed Al Franken's old *Saturday Night Live* skits as Stuart Smalley. I imagined him saying, "And gosh darn it, I love myself" as I said, "Look at my boobs and relax." Science research *does* say that boobs are physiologically relaxing to gaze upon. The idea of a meditation video with rhythmic boob squishing and calming directives to breathe just cracked me up. It wasn't a direct spoof of Al Franken, but an homage of the heart.

Now I'm saying that dumb shit for real. And I hate it. It's embarrassing. I shouldn't have to love myself. Other people should do it.

I'm afraid some people are going to hate me, like burn-my-books hate me. Or worse, freeze-my-bank-accounts hate me. This masturbation project is just the beginning. I'm deconstructing sex and sexuality in ways that my dad would definitely define as witchcraft.

Fuck.

"I love and accept myself, just the way I am."

I say it every week. And tears stream down my face.

I thought filming the project would be the hard part. It's not. That was nothing. Writing the project is fucking killing me. It should be the easy part. I have an MFA in creative writing, for Christ's sake. I had no training in filmmaking. But writing this, I have to reexamine the experience of filming. I record the parts that were scary, the parts I liked, what turned me on, what surprised me, what was problematic, who I imagined, how I felt, what problems got in the way, or what awesome thing I discovered about myself.

I think of different prospective readers and what they might need to understand and use the experiences I've had.

Kink and sex can be really scary for people. I was surprised to find my work triggered even a few experienced kinksters I know. They were triggered by things I thought were relatively benign, that I still think are relatively benign. My work is just an earnest attempt to render my emotional experience into artistic form. It's never my desire to harm or scare anyone, but people are complicated, and there's no way to guarantee there won't be folks who wish they'd never read what I wrote, or worse.

"I love and accept myself, just the way I am."

Good God. I love and fucking accept that I have daddy issues, that I dress up like a little girl to be sexually provocative and that I am an exhibitionist.

"I love and accept myself, just the way I am."

Fucky, fuck, fuck.

I cry and cry some more.

I don't want to love me. It's too hard. It's too scary.

I stop posting to social media. If I don't publish my book, there's no point in having fans. I don't want anything if I don't write my book.

My credit card processing goes down. The website is flagged as high risk, again. In a year and a half, I had exactly zero chargebacks or complaints. That's a damn good record, I think. No such thing as an ethical business involving sex, according to Mastercard and Visa. I don't even bother trying to fix it. I need to write. No distractions.

Since no money is coming in, I stop posting videos. I did six months more than I'd intended simply out of uncertainty over how to end it.

I'm still paying for hosting, website, email management, tech support and now there is no money coming from the website. It's become an ongoing expense. I loan myself the funds to float the website until the book is done too. It's an investment, just like my education, I tell myself. This is a small debt compared to college, and it's totally worth it.

Oh my God, but what if it's not? What if I'm a shit-for-brains delusional loser?

I'm not going to listen to that nasty talk. I put on another inspirational audiobook.

My therapist asks what my life was like when I was five. *Flashdance* was my favorite movie when I was five. I used to dance to the soundtrack. The rooms I danced in at that age were living rooms at friends' houses. I didn't like those friends. My dad hated those friends. Those were people who brainwashed my mom into leaving my dad. We stayed with them while my mom looked for a place for us to live after the divorce.

I'm stunned. I'm still in utter shock. I hear these childhood thoughts spoken aloud and realize what a load of shit my dad was feeding us kids. He made his children homeless. We stayed with "friends" because we didn't have anywhere else to go. Our town was too small for a battered-women's shelter. They weren't our friends, they were community volunteers, I realize as my adult mind rewrites the past.

We were homeless, but I never used that word because we weren't under an overpass or sleeping in a car. We were homeless, but I never thought of it that way. I buried it under nicer words. How could I have been unaware of such a basic fact about my childhood? It's as if I told myself it didn't happen. It is a fact. I experienced homelessness as a child and I totally fucking suppressed it. I experienced homelessness because my dad was abusive.

Tears stream down my face.

"Look around and see that you are now safe. Whatever you thought was going to happen to you if you didn't please others back then, you can let it go. They were real fears then, but now you are grown and strong. Can you show that little girl how well you've done for yourself, how strong you've become? Thank her for keeping you safe, and show her that her fear and alarm aren't needed anymore," my friend says.

"I love and accept myself, just the way I am."

Good God, I really hate this work, but it's helping.

I start writing again.

I hire a writing coach. She's amazing. She's just the right balance of encouraging and understanding. Just knowing that I'm going to talk to her helps me get a few extra pages in each week. I'm pretty sure the universe invented her just for me, because she's just who I need in my life right now.

I write.

Tears stream down my face. I can't believe I masturbated for a whole year thinking that I was learning how to be shameless in my sexuality.

I was learning to love myself. Literally.

And it fucking sucks.

24

a gift to the world

"MOM, PUT YOUR EARRINGS ON," my daughter urges. "The math ones."

"After my shower," I tell her. I know she has a reason for wanting me to put them on. I can't imagine what it is. They are a lovely pair of silver Möbius strips. I've worn them to every math conference I've presented at. I love them unreasonably. Mathematically, a Möbius strip is a one-sided nonorientable surface. To me it's part of the puzzle of infinity, a two-sided loop with only one surface. You can circle the inside and outside of the loop forever, without ever lifting from its surface. I wish I had a deeper mathematical understanding.

I'll put them on later. The best part of Christmas is staying in pajamas all day.

We scramble eggs for breakfast and eat them with Brie and pesto. Food is the center of merriment in our household. I'm not cooking some crazy-big Christmas dinner, just gonna throw some pork and sweet potatoes in the oven, easy peasy lazy meezy. I've splurged on the other foodstuffs I haven't been able to justify in a while, like a nine-dollar jar of my favorite hot dilly beans and a big log of goat cheese.

While my daughter was still sleeping this morning, I snuck out and unwrapped a gift I'd stuck under the tree myself. A year and a half ago I filmed a masturbation video in Mexico wearing a chastity belt, seeing if I could have an orgasm despite its hindrances. I could. But it was a crappy orgasm and left me with a frustrated, "That's it?!?!?"

But I was happy. Who else gets to run sexual experiments on themselves in paradise and then share them with the world? I'm a lucky, lucky woman. I had palm trees outside the window and an ocean view. It was an enchanted week with churros on a moonlit beach and fresh-fruit margaritas.

This year I got a new chastity belt. When it arrived two months ago, I couldn't even open it. I was scared I'd gained too much weight and it wouldn't fit. Steel is an unforgiving medium. I couldn't handle it. And I didn't even want it. Not anymore.

My last boyfriend was into degradation and humiliation, covert and nonconsensual. In other words, he was emotionally abusive. And he was extraordinarily entitled when it came to my sexuality. He acted like I was crazy when I said no or tried to protect myself.

And still I loved him.

It was painful.

I don't ever want to give my sexual agency away again, not in any way. Not after standing up in court to get a restraining order and having him say, "But she likes it that way. Look at her blog."

I own my sexuality. I defended my right to say no in a court of law. I can't put some chastity belt on and pretend like someone else owns me. Not even for fantasy. I imagine scenes that would have once turned me on. I script things in my mind that would make me money, but I can't just film any old crap. I do want to make money, but I want to make it doing remarkable things. The world doesn't need another woman pretending to be what men want. The world needs me. I am a writer, an educator and an indie porn producer. I'm a mother. I'm a woman. And my work involves finding female pleasure in sexual shamelessness. And it is work.

That's the lecture I give myself every time my eyes fall on the unopened box in the corner of my bedroom. I don't have a clue how to find my pleasure in the midst of all these competing agendas. The guy who sent it to me, I promised him I'd make a video with it.

I haven't.

That makes me feel shitty, because I think of myself as a woman of her word. But I haven't been able to do it.

He has been so sweet about it. No pressure. I am so grateful. I told him I was dealing with a lot, and depressed. But it's frustrating, so frustrating. I dedicated months of my life to pleasing an asshole boyfriend, and getting used by him. And then I'm flaking out on a nice guy.

How stereotypical.

Life is not that bad when you're up at night feeling guilty for not playing with your fancy new sex toys, I tell myself. But guilt is guilt, and I only half listen.

After a chat with this guy last week, where I dodged questions about the film I promised, I woke with an idea. I'd use the belt to lock my sexuality up as mine. I'd hold the key. In the future, I'd unlock my sexuality only on my terms.

A bunch of ideas for power-reversal chastity porn flooded

my mind. I need a camera crew to get all this shit filmed. I told the guy about my ideas the next morning.

"I've never heard of anything like that," he said. "You have to do it."

"I know," I told him. "I just have to finish my book first."

My book still isn't "done" but it has been through the first trip to the editor. And I'm finally in an emotional equilibrium that's left room for opening the box that holds the chastity belt that's been hanging over my head for months.

Late last night, Christmas Eve, I wrapped it up as a present to myself.

I woke just before dawn and set up my cameras. With my daughter now seventeen, I don't have to worry about her running into the living room to pounce on her stocking. She sleeps until ten. Besides, I wasn't going to masturbate. I was just going to open the box. And try it on. She's walked in on me doing sillier stuff than that. Like that time I was doing a pumpkin-carving photoshoot and had to beg her to bring me a towel after because I hadn't thought through how to get from the living room to the bathroom with seeds stuck all over my naked silliness. She laughed at me and brought two towels. Even with the towels, I left a trail of big fat pumpkin seeds from the living room to the bathroom.

I opened the box slowly, getting plenty of footage of the tape splitting under the pressure of the scissor's edge. The belt looked huge and so empty. I flushed with embarrassment at being such a big girl, but I didn't dwell on it. I filmed the key fitting into the lock, and I turned it slowly. I stepped into the contraption and I got the best Christmas present ever. The belt fit! And it looked amazing. I danced around the Christmas tree and watched the snow falling outside the window as dawn brightened into morning. It took me a spell of fumbling to figure out how to lock myself into the contraption. I got it all on film.

I love my life.

I cleaned all that up long before my daughter woke and made a cup of tea. We ate, opened our stockings and are going for a walk. We aren't opening presents until my mom arrives this afternoon.

We walk in the snow, by the frozen lake, trench coats over our pajamas. The blue sky is so beautiful, I don't care about the nostril hairs freezing together in my nose. The tromp, tromp, tromp of our snow boots leaves a tale of a trail, two intrepid wanderers braving the wilderness for some extra holiday joy. It warms my heart, even as my nose starts to run.

We do the short loop.

"Mom, put your Möbius earrings on," my daughter says again after our walk.

"Okay," I say. But I get distracted.

My mom arrives early. My ears are unadorned, and I'm still in cozy pajamas as I curl up in the soft chair next to the tree so we can open the last of the Christmas presents.

"This one is from both of us." My daughter proudly hands me a shiny red gift bag.

"Thank you," I say.

Under three layers of tissue paper there's a small white box with the word *Crave* embossed in gold on the front. I should know what this is, but I don't. My brows are doing their furl-in-confusion thing. I slide the box out of its cellophane wrapper. It hinges open like a jewelry box; it's the right size for a bracelet.

"Oh my God, it's that vibrator necklace!" I exclaim. I'd never have guessed.

"Yes," my daughter says, beaming with pride. "To go with your earrings."

"It's a matching set for my two careers, math-teacher Möbius-strip earrings and a porn-star vibrator necklace." I say this out loud to verify that I understand her perfectly, and I think she's brilliant.

"Yes!" she says, nearly bouncing out of her seat in excitement.

I'm tearing up. I can feel the little glands at the corners of my eyes doing their thing.

"Mormor helped pay for it," she explains. "Do you like it?"

"I love it." There's a second when the five unopened vibrators and sex toys in my closet flash through my mind. I'm not big on doing toy reviews. But my daughter and mother didn't buy me a vibrator to review. My daughter picked out a necklace to match my favorite earrings. My daughter bought me something to wear with pride, something that represents who I'm becoming. And it matches who I've been.

I blink back the tears.

"It's perfect," I say.

EPILOGUE

BEFORE THIS PROJECT I didn't use porn to masturbate. I do now. I no longer feel icky or scared watching porn. If I don't like what I find, I look for something else, as casually as I would with any other movie. There are lots of movies I don't like, with topics that scare me. Sex is no longer one of them.

This week I masturbated, twice. Both were quickies. A little anime porn, my Hitachi, an orgasm and I was out for the night. On the one hand I wonder about the metaphysical ramifications of the fact that my masturbation practice is now rather ordinary, and quite literally puts me to sleep. On the other hand, I could never have had a quickie before writing this book, because the hurdles of fear and shame were too high to jump so casually.

My favorite way to masturbate is still on film, but like ice cream and champagne, there's a time for that, but it ain't every night.

ABOUT THE AUTHOR

JUPITER'S SLUT is a writer, humorist and an accidental porn star. She prides herself on her fluency with two of the scariest words in the American dialect: math and porn.

Jupiter holds a Master's in Education from UMass Amherst and one in Creative Writing from Simmons College. She graduated with honors from Smith College with a self-designed major in economics and ethics. She does not represent herself as an authority in either math or porn but as a lifelong learner who strives to empower others as she empowers herself.

For the first thirty years of her life, Jupiter was math phobic and sexually repressed, and did not identify as a feminist. Growth in all areas of her life stemmed from stepping closer to her fears and pursuing joy. Through her work, she gives others the permission to play and the tools to revise their own lives.

You can find her writer's website at jupitersslut.com and the videos from the Masturbation Monday project at masturbationmonday.com.

THANK YOU

Honest, authentic reviews, written by real readers impact book sales. If you love this book, please review it.

www.ingramcontent.com/pod-product-compliance
Lightning Source LLC
Chambersburg PA
CBHW020413080526
44584CB00014B/1314